Spiritual Life
Coaching

Thelma P. Brown

© Thelma P. Brown 2007
Spiritual Life Coaching

ISBN 978-0-9559286-0-4

Published by
Primrose Publishing
20 Shand Park
Axminster
Devon
EX13 5NG

A CIP catalogue record of this book
can be obtained from the British Library.

Book designed by Michael Walsh at
THE BETTER BOOK COMPANY
A division of
RPM Print & Design
2-3 Spur Road
Chichester
West Sussex
PO19 8PR

CHAPTERS

LIST OF PROJECTS

FOREWORD

Some years ago I went through a traumatic experience that changed my whole world, Nothing made any sense. Anything that I could think of to do with my life seemed pointless and useless, I did not contemplate suicide as that is not in my makeup, but I did throw my concept of God out of the window (so to speak).

Nothing, but nothing that I had experienced concerning life and God had prepared me to be able to cope with the dreadful emotional suffering I was going through. However, after I had denied and decried God thoroughly, I realised that I was still getting nowhere fast.

Into my misery crept a thought – well maybe a 'sensing' would be a better word. A sensing that there just HAD to be more to life than I had found out about up to that point in time. There had to be more reason for life, more fairness to life and more motivation for life. There just had to be!

Somewhere I have read 'As you seek so shall you find', I began to seek, almost blindly, as I had no idea what I was searching for. Yet almost immediately I began to be given answers. Answers that were to transform my life so completely as to seem like a miracle, I was not perfect in my searching; the answers were not always easy to comprehend. There was also a kind of relationship with God to explore and experience that I had certainly never dreamed of.

This book is the result of some of the things that I have experienced over the past few years. It is offered with love and a hope that it might act like a finger pointing a new path of understanding, both of life and death, that you never realised existed.

CHAPTER ONE
Your Hidden Value

THE CANDLE

I had a little candle,
Only one I fear.
And when it was lit,
The light was not too clear.

Then I gave another candle
To a friend I knew.
When I lit her candle for her,
Why my little light grew.

The we each gave a candle,
To a friend in need.
With our four candles burning,
Was planted a seed.

If we four gave a candle,
And so on and so forth.
In a very short time,
We could light up the earth.

So never again say,
For you there is no place.
Help to light candles,
Bring a glow to a face.

Know how much you are needed,
Your value and your worth.
For the candles you light,
Reflect Heaven on Earth.

'Spiritual Life Coaching' is a teaching programme designed to open you up to an awareness of your value, your worth and your importance to yourself, to humanity and to God.

Through the teachings will be created a self-actualizing group of people who will live out, in their everyday lives, the precepts that will be offered. These precepts are offered to humanity regardless of race, creed or colour. All who come needing help, or looking for a deeper meaning to life are welcome.

It is not intended that you should just come and listen or just read this book. That is only a part of it. The most important part is that you should accept the reality of being able to 'listen inwardly', finding new values concerning yourself, and thus learning that you have the authority to help others in a similar manner. It is just a matter of being shown the potential you have within yourselves, experiencing it and then going on to share it. That potential already exists within you. The ideas in the book will search it out and bring it to life.

It will not consist of a leader standing up and telling you exactly what you ought to do or ought to believe. You may take the ideas and try them out or not, as you wish. However, be clear about this. Although everything is a thought first, nothing will be achieved if the thoughts stay on the shelves of your mind. You may know the techniques for skating, but until you get out on that ice and try it for yourself you will never learn how to skate.

If you want to achieve anything from this course, try not to act like many students at school do. They begin a course, even attend the classes spasmodically, but never get around to doing their homework. The homework is as equally important as the classwork, maybe even more so. You need to experience first-hand. Many students have failed an examination simply because they were not prepared to discipline themselves to do their homework.

This book could change the whole concept of your life, and that is almost an understatement.

Everything that is offered in 'Spiritual Life Coaching' has been tried out and experienced in life and found to work, yet still it is only offered to you. The challenge is for you to experience it and thus prove to yourself and to your own satisfaction that up until now, your self-evaluation was far, far too low.

Have you ever given any thought as to how valuable you might or could be? Is there any sense to your life? What is the purpose of it all? Why this effort to be born, to grow up, to raise a family, only to grow old and die and sink into obscurity, unless you are the very rare person who seems to do or say something that leaves a sense of immortality behind? So what is YOUR rating of value?

If there is a God and He is supposed to be a good God, then why does He allow so much misery and suffering? Why do some people get too much and others not enough? Why are some pretty enough to get married and feel the warmth of love and others not pretty or handsome enough to appeal to anyone?

So many of you have questions like these inside yourselves and are afraid to come out into the open with them, or feel that if you do question these things, there is no one who can answer with any degree of knowledge, understanding, clarity and a 'knowing'. Yet, as you have the courage to question and search for laudable answers, so they will begin to come, they MUST come.

Do you feel like a free person? Maybe you belong to a free nation, but that is not quite the same as being a free person. A free person, a really free person, is not always discernible to the outward eye. It is not necessarily someone without family responsibilities, with plenty of means of financial support, or with plenty of time to do anything or go anywhere.

A person like that can be no more free than you are. Can be a slave like you are. A slave to what? A slave to habits. Slaves as to how to dress, how to eat, or overeat, slaves as to what to say, slaves to your reactions to what other people say. There is even slavery to religion Maybe that is the strongest one of all, because that is often a slavery to fear.

We also let ourselves become slaves as far as our value is concerned. Early on in life we listen to casual comments about ourselves from others and eventually we accept them as truth. We cannot sew, or we cannot cook, or we are not very brainy, We have a temper or we cannot slim. We cannot learn a language or we are not very lovable. (When I was about nine years old, I wrote in an essay at school that I was not lovable because I had a snub nose!)

Who sets all the barriers? WE DO. Many of these things we could alter or learn if we really wanted to. We just need the incentive to know that these values are already in us.

"What qualifications do you have?" How many times in your life have you heard those words or words similar to them. I was asked that question many times when I first put forward the idea of a Slimming Class – the first in the country. I gave the very honest answer that I had served an apprenticeship of fifteen years, studying everything from magazines to books to tablets from the doctor, to try and get slim. Eventually I did a pilot scheme with an acquaintance (not a close friend) over the telephone for a year and it worked, using a 'no forbidden foods diet' or rather a 'no forbidden foods eating plan' approved by a London nutritionist.

So, how many of you have come to accept that in order to be acceptable to society you MUST conform, must NOT ask questions? Maybe the security that comes with conforming is what many need. But what is being lost at the same time? A sense of being an individual, of being a free person inwardly, a person with something unique to give, something of value that someone else has not given. How many people look, act and even feel like cardboard people? Yet, the potential is there for an 'inner freedom' if you will have the courage to look for it.

Each person is like a seed; each with a fantastic potential within. You are a valuable commodity in this world and most of you are quite oblivious to that fact.

Try to find a quiet spot and a quiet time to ask yourself the following questions.

1. Are you 100% content?
2. Do you enjoy your work?
3. Do you have a good relationship with other people?
4. Do you know why you are alive?
5. Do you know what life is really all about?
6. Are you in control of your life, or is your life in control of you?
7. Do you feel needed?
8. Do you feel valuable?

Try not to feel miserable if some of your answers are negative, but find a bit of paper and pen or pencil and now let your mind be quiet and receptive and concentrate on letting a letter from Jesus (as your brother) come through to you. It may be short, it may be long, in may be in the form of poetry or even a picture as well. It may come easily or it may come with difficulty, or even cause tears.

The important thing is to EXPERIENCE this and not to have preconceived ideas as to what Jesus might write to you, or thoughts such as 'Why would Jesus consider writing to ME?' Just try!

I am sure that many, many of you have been very pleasantly surprised. Some of the letters might be really short, some will have PSs to them. So far, with all the letters we have shared, none has ever been negative. All have been amazingly pertinent to each person. Many have found that they have felt impelled to sign the letter from 'Your loving brother Jesus' or similar.

There was a question that was often asked – "How do I know that the letter really was from Jesus?" I would like to reply with another question "How did the letter make you feel?" Even if you think it must have been your imagination, doesn't it feel great to have such an imagination and again – How did it make you feel? This is a really unique experience.

To those of you who could not get anything, don't give up. Try again and again and do not think that you are not worthy or not good enough to receive anything. Let Jesus surprise you. (Whatever or however you conceive him to be.)

I think it is important to emphasise how positive the results from this project were. The results from a class I did in America give some examples. In this instance the people actually did this project at home and then brought the results to class to share (or not share) with others.

I think amazement and wonder was the predominant look on their faces. The results were so personal and often not at all what had been expected. Some people very deep in a particularly troubling time were given comfort, support, understanding and courage. Some people were able to release a lot of negative feelings with poems, one person even got music.

Jesus did not seem to be concerned as to exactly who or what each person thought about him, he seemed to be a fountain of simple loving kindness, trying to heal each person in some way.

He was not interested in what they thought their faults were, just so pleased they had tried to open themselves up to him. It also turned out that he was quite happy to write to them again and again if they so wished. Always in a positive mood. Nice isn't it?

* * * * *

7

COURAGE

If I should find
I am needed by God,
Will I sit right there
Or start to plod?

If folk laugh at me
Or fill me with fear,
Will I turn and run
Or stay right there?

The man God sent
Called Jesus the Christ:
Was he ALWAYS acknowledged
Or considered right?

I think the next verse
With its simple lines,
Might give us courage
For the tougher times.

When the day has come
That you have died,
Will they say you failed
Or that you tried?

* * * * *

PROJECT

Find a time when you can be alone for a little peace and quiet. Get a pen and a blank sheet of paper. Let your mind be quiet and receptive and concentrate on getting a letter *from* Jesus (as your brother.) It may be short, long, flow easily, come with difficulty or even cause you to cry. It may be in the form of a note, a poem or even a musical message. The important thing is to EXPERIENCE it for yourself, openly, and not have preconceived ideas at to what might come.

CHAPTER TWO

Why Are You Here?

Shall we look a little more closely at this thing called 'Life'? Exactly what is it all about? Why are we here, or do we think it is just by chance? All a casual accident? If we think that way, how individual or special do you think you are? Are you living or are you rather like an automated puppet? Just sit and think about your idea very seriously for a few moments. Do you ever try and think thoughts of your own, or do you just go along with the crowd? What if we found out that there was a purpose to our life? A reason for being here that we had not known of before? Might that not make a difference to our outlook? Supposing we found out that everything, but everything that happens to us, good or bad or indifferent was instigated by us? Does the idea please you or terrify you? How do you feel about taking such responsibility?

There is a simple law that exists. A natural law of 'Cause and Effect' or sometimes called 'Karma'. A simple law that says that every thought and every action of man or woman has a natural reaction. A non-belief in this law can occur when a person does not know also of the law of reincarnation. That which is done in one lifetime may not be reflected back until a later lifetime.

So it is as well to know that life is for learning. Like children we cannot be forced to learn the lessons, but know this: they will be given again and again until we do learn them. The choice is always ours. Remember also that all lessons are not painful. Some are very pleasant. As we sowed, so are we reaping. If you kick a cat, somewhere, sometime, you MUST suffer the pain you gave the cat. But equally if you stroke the cat and give it pleasure, somewhere, sometime you must receive a similar pleasure in kind. That is a law that exists – a natural law.

It does not mean that you come back as a cat, simply receive in kind what you gave out. This law of 'cause and effect' is otherwise known as 'Karma'. Whether you like it or not, believe in it or not, agree or not, every action you 'take in thought, word or deed has a reaction. It is perfectly balanced and has no favourites. It always works both ways, in that every bit of kindness you put into a day, at some time or the other, rebounds back, as will every last ounce of cruelty, be it with fist or tongue.

It will not do to be sweet and sugary if underneath the exterior, our interior is seething with anger. If the anger is justified then there is nothing wrong with that. (Even Jesus was known to lose his temper.) The idea is to treat everyone else exactly as we would like to be treated ourselves, simply because this what eventually happens.

This knowledge and understanding, together with a sensible outlook and understanding of reincarnation (that we live more than one life) can make perfect sense of all that comes to us in life. At last we will know that we MUST accept responsibility for our lives, for the ups and downs. All is meant to be, nothing is by chance, nothing by accident.

Some Christians may say that any talk of Karma (law of cause and effect) does not exists in the Bible, but mention is made of 'sowing and reaping', of talents being used and of expecting to be treated by life as we treat life.

Even more than the mention of 'Karma', the mention of reincarnation can cause heads to shake in disbelief. The following are worth checking out in the Bible:

Malachi   4: 5
Proverbs   8: 22-51
Matthew   11: 11-15
Matthew   16: 15 – 15
Matthew   17: 9-13

Luke   9: 7-9
John   8: 56-59

All is meant to teach us to teach ourselves. If we are deliberately selfish, it will be returned to us sooner or later. However, if we give freely, we seem to be given back more than that which we gave. Something is added to it. First we get the pleasure of giving, then we get the pleasure of the other person reflected on to us. With this kind of philosophy you just cannot lose.

When the rough events come along you will look at them with different eyes. You will know that what you are having to endure is something that you yourself created with some past action, maybe many lives ago. Feeling resentment that you cannot remember, will not alter what is happening one iota.

As soon as you accept that you are paying a debt and try to see what you are to learn from it and do so willingly, much of the pain will disappear, The incident will not be able to have the same affect on you. You will begin to take charge, to look for the needed lesson and try to learn it as quickly as possible. As a teacher teaches two and two are four until the pupil learns thoroughly, so it will be with you. But you can rest assured that once you have faced the lesson, even with the pain, and accepted the understanding then the lesson will be finished and you can move on again.

Remember always, as you are meeting *krma* (past karma) on a day to day basis, so you are always creating your fresh karma. You are actually writing out invitations to future events. What kind of events do you want to attend?

Your first task here on earth, apart from being reunited with God, is self-improvement. If you will work at that to begin with, slowly and patiently, you will be shown and given opportunities to help others. Just as soon as you are ready.

Self-improvement. The word smacks of another word. Self-discipline. Yet could not self-discipline be a friend instead of an enemy? How many people like themselves? Really like themselves? The answer is understandable because we are not very often truthful about ourselves. We must give ourselves a balance sheet. We are all greater people than we have any idea of. Why not accept that fact and enjoy it. You do not have to fret or rush around so that others may feel the breeze of your existence. The sky stands still yet everyone looks at it every day.

You may need, for the time being, an exterior guide. Take any religion and look into the heart of it. If you really do that, you will find a thread of truth running right through the middle of it, no matter how much mumbo jumbo may have been stuck around the outside of it. Once you can see the golden central thread, your understanding will widen immediately. This link that is in all religions, the golden thread of truth, is pure Love that has nothing whatsoever to do with belief or disbelief.

If you can find it, then you will 'know'. By the way that 'knowing' is closer than any religion. It is right there sitting inside you, each and every one of you, just waiting to be acknowledged!

You may have found that you are here to learn. That you are here to be tested with lessons. But you are also here to grow. To grow strong by taking new action, by doing new things, by thinking new ideas.

So what do we fear? Our own fears. Our own failures. Yet without action nothing is achieved. Remember, nothing ventured, nothing gained. Today will be the same as yesterday and tomorrow will be the same as today, unless YOU make it change. Not necessarily big changes. Not necessarily a change of job or home or wife.

The changes must come from your attitude to these things. Most people have an automatic reaction to life. They will complain about the weather whatever it is. In a likewise manner they will complain about their lives.

They complain about the neighbours and they complain about the government. They complain about their car and about their children. They are not happy, and, yet it is not always for the reason they like to give. First of all they are not happy with themselves and so they project it on to someone or something outside of themselves. This way they do not have to accept the responsibility for their unhappiness. They can then act as if they are puppets with no minds or willpower to change what they do not like.

They try to say "Look how the world treats me – what it does to me" In effect they are saying "Look how I react to the world and its ways." Only you can take the necessary action to change things. Your whole world can turn around, simply by you first of all turning your attitude around. Try it!

Try an experiment. For just one week look honestly and without judgment at your reaction to events.

If you become angry over something the children or family or friends do, stand back and have a quiet look at what the anger is all about. Really all about.

If you are worrying about something, take the worry to its logical conclusion and see what action you would have to take, if the worry ever happened.

Finally, if you feel especially happy, what was necessary for the happiness. Let there be no guilt, or anxiety or judgment about this week's experiment. Simply observe.

WHY?

Has no one ever told you
The reason you are here,
Why the smiles and the laughter,
Then the pain and the fear?

Has no one explained
What you are here to do,
That life has a purpose,
An understanding for you?

If you live one life,
And one life you die,
Then there is no sense
To this strange bye and bye.

But if each 'life' is different
And you're no fool,
Think on this one then –
Life is like a school.

The one who comes to this school
Is a creature strange, not rare;
A soul just masquerading
As a man, or woman fair.

A soul that needs the lessons
Only school of life can show,
Yet has to be a prisoner
Till the ego lets it go.

There is nothing by chance,
Neither shame, nor fame;
We were the diviners –
Our arrows took aim.

We may not remember
The time nor the place,
When we wrote our plans,
Chose our future space.

Yet the ones we have wronged
Come to meet us again,
And now is the time
To undo our shame.

The ones we love
We have loved before,
Many times ago
In days of yore.

So why not use this lifetime?
Don't accept or fret –
You are here for a purpose,
For a chance at which you leapt.

See what life dishes out
With different eyes,
All is done for a purpose,
Not just 'pie in the sky'.

If maybe different lessons
Are what you need to learn,
Watch carefully what you get,
And learn to discern.

Keep an open mind,
And an open heart too,
So when tests come along
You know just what to do.

Know this to be true
Without shadow of doubt,
We only suffer
When our conscience we flout.

Two and two are four –
We'll be tested once more
When the lesson is learned;
We can then close the door.

Till we can move on
To another class,
An understanding grows,
And our tests we pass.

And the day must come
When our schooling is done,
We can shut the books,
And return to our Home.

(This poem reflects Chapter Two – *Why Are You Here?*)

PROJECT

Try and look honestly and without judgment for a whole week at your *reactions* to events that you respond to emotionally. See if you can stand back and relax your attitude more.

CHAPTER THREE
The Rebirth Of You

In the previous chapter you were asked to look at things that depressed you, at things that angered you, things that worried you and things that made you happy. What did you find?

I would like to say a few words on 'Happiness'. Have we the courage to look at 'happiness' and decide what constitutes it? Today, for a woman, it may mean the birth of her first baby. In a few years time it could mean the first day that the same little baby (now a demanding, energy-consuming, ever-questioning, fizzing five-year-old) goes off to school.

'Happiness' today for a sixteen-year-old may mean receiving a very special love letter. In five years time it may mean receiving divorce papers. For a man it may be receiving his degree at college and ten years hence it may be the morning he walks out of the office and the rat race to become a 'responsibility-free' labourer.

We should learn to see how ethereal happiness is. Likewise with depression or anger or worry. Time is always passing and circumstances are always changing, so what contentment can we find in each day.

If you had bare feet you would long for shoes. If you had shoes and no socks you would long for socks to make them more comfortable.

So the man with feet and shoes keeps longing for socks instead of being grateful that he has feet to put the shoes on to. There is nothing wrong with striving for more, but at the same time look to see what you already have.

If the outer circumstances are always changing how can we improve things. Maybe managing to be more of an observer than just a participant and introducing a different attitude? The attitude you give out is the attitude that will be returned to you sooner or later. Remember, you are writing your own play with you as the lead actor or actress. Do you maybe feel a bit lost with the idea that you are just you, all on your own with no special qualifications to justify your ability to change things. But you are not really alone and you have unknown potential just sitting inside you.

The following was given to me one morning as I sat meditating :-

God's Shiny Eyes

Once upon a time there was just God. A great God, the one and only God. Neither a man or woman, but rather like an angel, but without any wings.

Now this was no ordinary being, because He was made up of all the things in the whole world and even beyond. The beyond was at the back of Him, where the planets and galaxies exist that we cannot see.

His legs were all the trees in the world and His feet the soil, while His toes consisted of the little creatures who live underground. His toenails shone with the different jewels of the world, and around His feet lapped all the oceans, with the sea creatures swimming in them.

Just above His head were beautiful skies which the clouds floated in, together with the sun, moon and stars, while His hair consisted of all the birds in the whole world.

Below His waist were the metals: iron, copper, steel and many more. Around His waist He wore a beautiful belt made up of all the animals, One arm consisted of all the flying insects and butterflies, whilst the other arm was green with grasses, and around it curved all the rainbows. His hands and fingers glowed with shrubs and flowers.

Just above His waist were all the mountains and hills, with the snow drifting around their peaks, while the lakes and streams flowed in the valleys. The seasons played games here, whilst waiting for their time to work to come around.

His ears were all the vegetables and His nose the scents and perfumes. His mouth sang all the songs and music of the whole world, whilst on His cheeks the colours moved to the sound of the music. His eyebrows were all the sunrises and sunsets.

But His eyes were the most wonderful of all. They shone with a strange light, a brilliant light that was brighter than the sun, yet not painful to observe. They glowed and glowed.

So God had everything and had nothing left to wish for. Yet He was not completely happy. One thing marred His joy. He had no one to share all these things with and He was lonely. No one existed but Himself and he felt a great longing for companionship.

Now there is a strange thing about companionship. In order to experience it, you have to be prepared to give of yourself. So it was with God. Even he could not have companionship without giving, and so He gave the most important part of Himself.

He took out of Himself his Soul, which was like a brilliant diamond to look at and yet was made of pure love. Trembling with excitement He shattered his Soul, His very being, into millions and millions of tiny fragments, each piece a perfect copy of His own original Soul. Only one piece He kept back for Himself, and the rest He gave away.

Now He gazed down at these millions of little beings with delight and anticipation, waiting for the expected companionship to begin. Suddenly He realised something. Rather than creating companions, He had created puppets. There was no original thinking or feeling. They acted and thought exactly as God did. They had nothing to give but a reflection, a copy. They were only like shadows.

So God sat and thought about the problem for a long time. There seemed to be only one answer and He knew that once that step was taken there was no turning back. Yet God had trust as well as love tucked away inside, and so with that trust He took that great step. He gave his offspring free will. In that way only, could they be real companions.

The choice is yours as to whether you believe my story or not, but hasn't it ever crossed your mind to wonder why people's eyes shine, especially if they care about you or love you? Also some animals' eyes?

It is but a reflection of the soul that God gave each one of you, shining through the windows of the body. Now you know why God has shiny eyes.

* * * * *

Reincarnation. The very word and the thought that it sight apply to each and everyone of us is enough to make some people shudder. They will say that this life has been so unpleasant that they do not want to accept the idea that they might have to experience another one like it. Or else they think they might have to come back as an animal next time. My soul has never accepted the latter idea.

If reincarnation existed without karma, then there might be some cause for fear, but with karma it has a sense of law and order and justice to it. How can we believe in God and especially a good God if we think that we only live one life? It makes a mockery of God to say that He lets us have enough to eat, a place to sleep, and a family to love, whilst other people have none of these things.

With the free will that God gave us, many of us chose to wander far, far away from Him and our real home. Now is the time to start to find our way back. Unfortunately, over the ages, we have cluttered our original pure vibrations up with hate, greed, envy and so on and so forth. This clouds us up so that we cannot see the lights of Home shining. Yet, even now, we see a faint glimmer and have started to follow it.

To return to the idea of reincarnation for a little longer. There are some very good books on the subject which you would do well to read, but this much more I would share with you.

(1) You asked to come back.

(2) Other souls also wished to do so, but there are always more souls waiting to reincarnate than there are places.

(3) You chose your parents! Interesting isn't it?

(4) You saw a blueprint of what it was that you hoped to achieve in this lifetime before you came back.

(5) If you learn to 'listen inwardly', you will get much soul guidance concerning the blueprint.

(6) When you die, you then get the chance to put the blueprint of your life along beside the original plan. Makes you think a little, doesn't it?

As you will begin to understand from the previous material, we each have a responsibility. Our lives were not given to us just to fritter away.

The best place for our soul to progress is on earth. As I said just now, there are more souls waiting to come back than there are places. If you have this chance then another soul has been denied that chance. Do not waste it. It is not only for your personal progress. It is so that you may, even if by example only, remind souls who have forgotten why they are here, what life is really all about.

It is, or it can be, a life of sharing. If we learn to listen well inwardly, we will be guided, when we are unsure of what action or reaction is for the best.

The following I found out almost by accident. I found that my meditation success depended on how I had treated my soul that day. If I had been wrong with my actions, (in

23

spite of my soul trying to talk with me (or might you call it your conscience?) Then when I came to have my evening talk with God (my Father or …) my soul would be the one that was suffering from my transgressions.

Not that God would not listen, but my guilty feelings would block the way, block the channel. So I would cry – or so it seemed, but eventually I realised that it was my soul crying as it was deprived of the communication it always so longed for. As always, the choice is always ours, but we must be prepared to stand by that and its consequences.

If we come to accept the fact of rebirth, then we must also realise that there have been many deaths. Even if we do not accept this premise, it is inevitable that we must face one death. The death at the end of this lifetime, or the death of loved ones.

Statistics show that a certain percentage of people are going to be involved in a car accident this year. We NEVER think that we will be one of those statistics. In the same way, we never allow ourselves to think of death, or if we do, it is usually with fear. So what do we fear? Well, sometimes it is fear of how the actual death will take place. What pain will be involved?

Cast your mind back to times in your life when you have had to undergo pain. Maybe having a baby, or going to the dentist, or breaking a leg etc. In all cases what happens is that you find the strength from somewhere to bear the pain because you do not have any choice. It comes and it goes. However, there is no guarantee that your death will be a painful one.

Once I was involved in quite a bad car accident. It involved my car being turned over and totally wrecked. Whilst the accident was actually taking place, there was no pain and no anxiety. Nothing was real. It was like being in a slow motion picture scene with no noise and no feeling, Others have told, me of similar incidents.

Fear Of The Unknown

What is more often feared as far as death is concerned is the fear of the unknown. Yet have you not, at some time in your life, had to go out into the unknown. To a new town, or a new school, or a new job, or a new country? Have you not sometimes found that the fear of that unknown was quite often unreal and that there was, in fact, nothing to fear?

If we have any faith at all in a God or a Great Being, or Something that keeps law and order in the Universe, knowing that It created us, could we not trust that at the point of death we will be cared for?

There have been some very authentic cases recently of people who have had a death experience and lived to tell about it. Read about some of them and let your inner feelings guide you as to how YOU feel about them.

This much I can assure you. When you die you lose your physical body and your sense of pain. But all else you keep. You are still you. This is a great shock to many. If you have a temper here, then you will still have it in the next sphere, but there, people will be able to steer clear of you and not be subjected to it as they are here on earth. You still have the same personality and the same characteristics. The next plane is only one plane removed from earth. Life has less tension, but also less chance for growth. That is why it is essential to make the most of this life.

Another very important point to remember is that you create, whilst you are here, the type of space you will occupy when you die. As Jesus said, "In my Father's house are many mansions." By your words, deeds, thoughts and caring of others in this world, you are building your house (figuratively speaking) in the next world. There is your free will again.

Why not look on dying as an adventure, knowing that you will meet your loved ones again, as you have met them many times before.

PLEASE NOTE – I feel very strongly right now that I need to put in an incident that happened to me in America a few years ago. Namely, why you should NOT contemplate committing suicide so as to hopefully get to see them sooner.

I was at a small house party in America and was introduced briefly to a young girl whose mother, sadly, had died recently. A few days later I was distressed to hear that she had tried to commit suicide, had been rescued in time, but was now in hospital and refusing to speak to anyone at all or do anything. That evening I was driving home for a coffee morning and became aware of the girl's dead mother in the car, speaking to me. She desperately wanted me to go and see her daughter and give her a message.

Early that same evening I went to the hospital and found the girl. I introduced myself as having met her at the party although I did not expect she remembered me. I asked her if she thought that by committing suicide she would see her mother again and be with her. The girl did not speak but just nodded in the affirmative. I went on to say that I had a message for her from her mother. First of all she gave me some personal information so that the girl would know I really had been talking to her mother. Her mother had then gone on to say that if her daughter had committed suicide she would not have been able to go where her mother was or have contact with her. She would still have lost her. She said that what her daughter could do was to sit quietly each day, maybe looking at a photo of her mother and thinking of her and try to sense her around her. A feeling of warmth, of comfort, of love. All or any of these things could happen. Then in time the daughter would feel strong enough to let her mother go, knowing for sure that when she did die naturally they would be together again.

The girl did not say a lot, but she thanked me for coming, shed quite a few tears and said she did believe what I had said and already sensed her mother there as we were talking.

I seem to have digressed a lot from where I was, but it felt very important to put it in NOW and I will be writing more about death and suicide in a later chapter.

I firmly believe that we are moving into an age where the veil between the two worlds is getting thinner. This understanding can be of great comfort, not only to you who have lost someone, but to those who are in spirit and are trying desperately to let you know that they are still alive and well, albeit without their cumbersome physical bodies.

THE LUCKY ONES

Blessed are we that seek and try
Answers to questions to find.
Blessed are we that struggle and strive
to SEE and not to be blind.

Blessed are we that strain our ears
New things for to hear.
And blessed are we when we understand
The understanding of why we are here.

Here to sing songs of a world unseen,
To bring laughter to tear-drenched faces,
To bring a warmth to an aching heart,
In the most unexpected places.

As we offer our help in the humblest of ways,
Chances are there for the taking.
As we heal with a glance, a touch, or a smile,
Our own healed future we are making.

* * * * *

PROJECT

Experience for yourself 'A Telephone Call To God'. Use your imagination as to where your telephone box is situated, what colours are in evidence and what time of day or night you make the call.

CHAPTER FOUR

Your Free Will

After having read about Karma and Reincarnation, some of you may be feeling a little bewildered about this area. What Free Will?

You may feel that in spite of being told that you had asked to come back to Earth, how could you have possibly agreed to such a difficult life? Then to know that you have created 'karma' that dreadful law of 'cause and effect', which seems to mean that even if you have been good so far in this life, you still might get some terrible things coming along. A new knowledge of all this can be a bit depressing at first.

Yet, and this is a big yet, look at it this way. Because of what you now know, you have the free will – all the free will in the world – first of all as to how you react to the difficult things that come along, and then secondly, how you create your future. Notice also, some of the really lovely or wonderful things that have been, or are in your life, which you also must have created in the past. Quite a thought isn't it?

It is time now it seems, for me to put in what I consider to be one of the most important parts of the whole book.

Telephone Call To God

I wish to share something with you that could have a great effect on your life. It is something I was given a few years ago by God and I feel it has a lot of value.

A friend asked me if I could tell her how to meditate and I said that I would type something out for her. As I sat down at the typewriter the following came swiftly. I knew that I was being given something very special, It combines both prayer and meditation and is a 'Telephone Call To God'.

What kind of relationship, if any, do we have with God? Could you maybe think of Him as a friend? So what is a friendship? When you meet with your friend you will probably tell all the news, problems etc., that have happened to you, including any good things too. Then what happens? It is the turn of the friend to have their say. Well then, how about this possibility of a friendship with God? Up until this point in time you may feel that you must go to church in order to meet Him. But if you do this, what often happens whilst you are there?

You say some prayers, sing some hymns, listen to religious readings and a sermon or a talk. Then you sing another hymn, make a brief acknowledgement to the whole thing and get up and leave. Where, in the whole hour, did God get a chance to get a word in edgewise? How much talking did you let Him do? How much time did the minister or vicar or whoever, give you time to really listen inwardly.

Right now the inner feeling might be one of slight embarrassment. Why on earth should God actually lower Himself to talk to *you*? What could He possibly have to say, except maybe to scold us. He doesn't have any needs does He? Or does He? Might we not be more important to Him than we give ourselves credit for? After all He did create us? What for, if we are not to have any importance?

Someone once said to me rather glibly: "We are expendable." My soul response was instant and positive. It poured into my physical being the words: "Only YOU can do the work God sent you to do." But if we never listen inwardly, how can we possibly know what it is that He wants us to do or even just be, what He wants to share with us. He wants us to be companions, not just puppets, so how about an experiment in faith. A telephone call to God.

First of all, sit yourself comfortably, either on a chair, on the floor or on the bed. It does not matter where as long as you can relax and forget your body. Shut your eyes and take a few deep breaths to help relax you.

Now – picture a very special telephone. A magic telephone. A telephone that is never busy. It can be what colour feels good to you. Now concentrate on this telephone as if you were about to make a normal call. Pick up the inner receiver and dial. The magic of this telephone is that you dial the words that to you represent God, whether it be God, Jesus, Buddha, a flower or whatever. As long as the number you dial represents in symbol God to you, then it will connect.

Listen intently for the receiver to be picked up. Acknowledge with whatever words feel good to you, as you would with your friend. Right now it is up to you to do the talking or the praying. You might like to think of talking as a friend would, not just listing all your wants, but sharing some of the good things of the day too. If you do ask for things believe that they are possible IF GOD WILLS IT. Believe that you will get an answer, but accept that the answer, in whatever form, is for your own eventual good and growth.

When you have finished your talking, quieten your mind down and concentrate even more. This is the time that God will speak to you. He has, on occasions, a very soft voice and unless you concentrate really hard you may miss hearing Him. It is not so much a question of seeing Him in a vision, or even of hearing Him speak physical words, it is more a sense of sensing Him.

Your part is really just to let go of all thoughts and problems, you are only required to relax completely and let go of all responsibility for everything. Nothing is important at that precise moment but to be receptive.

God's Line Is Never Busy

Now may be the time to imagine yourself in a special glass telephone box with your telephone. It is like a bubble of silence and although you cannot see the busy images of your thoughts you know that you cannot hear them. They will soon get tired of talking to a glass wall and will quieten down. Remember, do not get cross with them; just let them know you will attend to them in a little while. By the time you are finished, many of the troublesome thoughts will have gone away, tired of waiting.

After you have been quietly listening, you may be aware of a sense of tingling and warmth or you may find yourself moved to unaccustomed tears. The tears are something that could happen time and time again, even for some weeks, but do not be ashamed of them. They are simply a melting away of the dross that has collected around our awareness of our oneness with God. They are only healing tears.

After a period of time, which will alter as you alter your length and depth of meditation, you will gradually sense a withdrawing of the 'awareness' and a feeling, almost of reluctance, of coming back to earth again. Almost as though the telephone receiver had been replaced. The time has ended for this call.

God, as we all do, has His likes and His 'better likes' and one thing is for sure. He likes being called EVERY day, not when you just feel in the mood or have an extra special favour to ask of Him.

The time you take is never, never wasted. What time you give to Him is repaid over and over again. It is not so much what you actually experience whilst the telephone call is taking place, but what seems to happen to your everyday life. It is as though you are being given something that permeates through everything that you do and say in the outside world.

Another thing, as time goes on, weeks, months and years, you may begin to sense Him telephoning you at all odd times. In the office, or in the car, or just as you wake up in the morning. I call these times in the morning: 'As I awoke' times. Sometimes an idea, sometimes just a sentence. Always positive and trying to be helpful, if we will but listen. God is not just in the church, or even just out in the wide beyond. He is simply an 'inner' telephone call way. The line is NEVER busy and you can always call collect. Why not try it for yourself?

Use your imagination as to where your telephone box is situated. Maybe a bubble, a rainbow bubble with a mobile in it? Remember, the regularity is of importance. Be patient. Accept and don't expect. It is a real thing that you are attempting. For many of you it is new, so do not rush things.

One person I know who did it would not wait to see if God would speak to him – he did not think he was worthy. Let God be the judge of that. All of us are worthy. We are His children and a spark of Him is in us. I can assure you that you will find that God will always be delighted that you tried to contact Him and are giving Him a chance to talk for a change.

Our Choice

Life is what we make it! True or False? With the understanding that we now have, isn't it time we began to have the courage to look at our life as it is, decide whether or not we like it, know that WE make it for the future and will make it in the present, depending upon our attitude to it. Running away is not the answer.

Life always was and always will be a series of choices. If we learn to meditate, whose method do we choose? If we are fat, we have decided to put enough food in our mouths to become that way (Well – did anyone force-feed you?) If you want to stop smoking, yet do not, we have made the choice to carry on smoking. So, if we want to become disciplined, how do we go about it? Whose suggestion or suggestions do we accept? How can we go about getting more out of life? Are we just robots or do we want to come alive? In the setting of the experience we may have no choice, but in our reactions is every choice.

However, time is necessary for the strengthening of new choices. If a thing is rushed it is weak, like a flower or plant that is forced on too quickly. Yet again, will today be like yesterday and will tomorrow be like today and the day after tomorrow and so on? The choice is yours. Only YOU can change things.

Now that you know how your free will can work, you may want to make some changes. Be clear exactly why and what you are trying to change and that the goals you are setting are what your soul wants for you.

The freedom we are given is the freedom for expansion or otherwise, as we see fit. There is no force – ever. The only guilt we can feel will come from within ourselves. Likewise the only progress we can make is from within ourselves. Within ourselves sits our true self, which speaks to us if we are to listen. Again, no force is used. If we wish to drown out the sound of our true self, this we may do. But do not blame God and weep at the results. The way will be shown if we wish it, but each must make and tread his own path. That is what makes us individuals. That is what we have our souls for. That is why God created us with a free will.

If all you look for in life is to eat, sleep, work and play, that is all you will get. Progress has to be looked for, really searched for and longed for. The payment is self. Self-discipline, self-awareness and self-knowledge. Even now, something inside you is trying to attract your attention in order to wake you up and in order to help you. Why not try listening?

EVOLUTION

At the end of the day when I sit to pray
And listen to God within,
Will my heart be glad, or truly sad
That my new day never began?

When I sat in the morn and watched the dawn
Then my aspirations ran high,
Now evening has come and the day is done
And my tears I sit down to dry.

What went wrong with today's new song,
How and why did I fail?
With my heaving chest and face all wet,
Like a child I bawl and wail.

At last the storm stops, although I've hiccups,
Now a voice speaks from within,
Who is condemning, who telling you off,
Who says that you have sinned?

That makes me think hard and I have to afford
That the judge and the jury is me.
No flaming sword, no fiery Lord,
Stood in anger for to see.

So a lesson I've learned, though the learning was heard,
That the choice is always mine.
To follow the me that sits within,
Or list to a different chime.

I can go as far as I truly dare,
No one will hold me back;
But I must be willing to accept the tasks
Along this special track.

When I have no fears, then very few tears
Will fall to blot the day,
And I will find joy to see the folk
That come to share my way.

* * * * *

PROJECT

Try another letter from Jesus. Surprised?

CHAPTER FIVE

The Power Within You

The Importance Of Self-Examination

Do not let the excuse of age deter you from trying to instigate changes in yourself. Obviously there are some physical changes that we can no longer suddenly do, that we did when we were younger. Often we are like a car or engine that has rusted up through lack of motion or lack of proper attention. Our beings reflect that, in the physical, mental and emotional and spiritual areas. All could stand an overhaul.

Self-examination of thoughts, emotions and actions. Why do you think and feel and act as you do? How much of it is automatic and routine? Something within you is suggesting that you are capable of being better than you are now. Achievement brings satisfaction. To prove not only to yourself that you are in charge, but to others as well. In all areas.

The aim is not necessarily greatness which could imply power, but fulfilment which implies contentment with what we cannot change and a willingness to work at changing that which can be changed. Daily regular effort would then be a pleasure as it shows up as an evolution of yourself. To be of value in the world, we can only offer as much as we are ourselves. That is the authority. Everything else we say and do shows up as false to the discerning people.

You really are worth studying. For until you learn to know yourself better, and why you react to certain things the way you do, and why you have certain feelings, it is going to be difficult to become the one who is in charge, instead of life being in charge of you.

So, consider yourself a subject to study, without guilt or rejection, or dislike or contempt, but almost as another being with much potential inside yourself.

(1) Write a letter to yourself, saying what is good about you. Go on. It won't hurt.

(2) Be your own analyst – in a positive way, not just negative.

(3) Look honestly at depression. Interesting area to look at here. Check out how much sugar you are eating! I have personal proof and further confirmation that sugar can make you feel depressed.

(4) You don't like your job. Then what are you doing to train yourself to do something you do like? What would happen if you changed your attitude even, especially if you are in contact with the public.

(5) You don't like certain people, I wonder what it is about them that you don't like? There is a theory that you can only see in someone what is in yourself. Think about it.

(6) How positive is your attitude to all your problems, or how negative? Look very carefully at that one. Remember, we create our own world.

This is to give you some idea of what you are trying to study. A subject more interesting, more fascinating and with more depth than anything else. YOURSELF!

Don't do something because you think you ought to do it. Don't try to be interested in something because you think it is the commonly done thing. Don't learn something because you feel it is information that others are learning and you should do the same.

Learn about something that feels right to you. Something that grips your imagination, that fires you with enthusiasm, that you can lose yourself in. Inwardly we all hope that we are special. We are – but usually we are too timid to tell ourselves what we would really like to hear. That we *are* worthwhile.

All our lives we look for approval. When we are little, our first memories are often of being cuddled or smacked. It seemed that if we conformed to what our parents wanted us to do, we could know they approved of us and this made us feel secure. If we tried to stick out for our own selves, then we would get smacked and even worse, feel their love was withdrawn, making us feel unwanted and unlovable. Much of that has gone on throughout the rest of our lives. We feel that only if we conform can we be loved. Yet know of this power within yourself. If you love first, with no strings attached, then love cannot but be returned. Remember, everything we do is reflected back sooner or later.

Most people are too nervous or too frightened to begin to think outside the narrow boundaries that have been set for them by other people from a very early age. So, when their lives are disturbed from their usual complacency, often the faith that they possess, is not enough to sustain them. They flounder and are not sure of their direction. If the God they have known up until then does not seem to hear them, then sometimes they will turn away altogether, feeling that God has failed them, when, in reality, they do not have a true understanding as to what God is really all about. Open your 'inner' eye.

A suggested project at the end of this chapter could be a very confronting, but very, very rewarding one for many of you. It is to take a relationship that exists in your life – a BAD relationship and begin to change it. Now the strange thing about a bad relationship is that many times we feel no guilt about it. We may even enjoy it saying "I cannot stand him or her because ..." We then go into a long list of justifications for not liking that particular person. But know this – whether you like it or not – it takes two to make a relationship – be it good or bad. If it is bad, then in some way, you are partially responsible for it.

Nasty thought isn't it – a bit uncomfortable – can't you just hear all the excuses just rushing to the surface as to why you are quite sure that it is not your fault in any way? Unfortunately, the truth is this that bad relationships exist because you have agreed that it shall be so, to yourself, even if not out loud. It is not suggested that you can completely change things overnight, but even in a week, you can if you choose, begin altering things – either with a letter, a telephone call, an e-mail, a smile etc., etc.

Remember this, that those so called enemies are people we have known before in other lives and they have come to meet us again, for whatever purpose. If we do not work those problems out now, then we are just putting it off for another day or another life. So why not start working on it now and get it over and done with.

Maybe you are hesitating and dithering a little at this stage. All this talk of a power within, but what qualifications do we have to be a recipient of such a power? So what qualifications do you need? A good, sound, deep experience of life and an even deeper understanding of the possibility of a living, down-to-earth positive relationship with God and with the Kingdom of God with all its great beings. The hierarchy that are there, just longing to give us a helping hand. Skill learning of any kind is accomplished only by trial and error. But an error is not necessarily a failure. It must be looked on for its learning possibility. Yes, look failure right in the eye and learn from it how to succeed. See what it is trying to teach you. You all have success already built into you. You would not be here today if it were not so. It is up to you to set it free. Instead of thinking what a failure you have been, in whatever area, begin thinking what a success you could be. After all, if God thought you were worth creating, He must have thought you were worth creating for something.

Everything is seen in the mind, no matter how swiftly, before it appears out in the world. Everything! So use the power within you to create what you want out of life. Remember, as you give out, so will you receive.

The previous ideas are not really stated in order to be argued about, but to think about. There are many things in life that we accept as a fact without trying to prove or disprove them, so why not accent the idea that there is a bit more to us than merely a bundle of flesh and bones with thoughts and feelings. Whilst life goes along smoothly and suits us, then this seems an easy idea to accept. But there may come a time in a man or woman's life when they feel a tremendous dissatisfaction with life and really begin to question what it is all about. Why should THEY have to be unhappy, lose their job, have their business fail, have the person they love die, be ill or leave them. Some people seem to have all the luck.

I will share a true story with you. Someone I knew in America said that all her life she had had a bad relationship with her father. What did I suggest that she do? I asked her if she had another relationship that was very good with another man, a friend or brother or husband or son. She said "Yes." I then suggested that she superimposed the loved one's face on her father's face the next time she spoke to him. That she spoke in a caring tone of voice as though she thought that her father really did love her and would not reject her loving advances. The father's reaction was very interesting. First he looked slightly bewildered and puzzled as if he thought his daughter was drunk or being sarcastic. Be he found that the approach was rather disarming so his grunted reply did not have its usual vehemence. In turn the daughter felt better and more relaxed and able to carry on with the experiment. After a few weeks the relationship was almost unrecognizable. Both father and daughter were much more at peace with each other and with themselves. No one really feels really good within themselves when there is strife in their lives. Maybe we cannot create perfect relationships, but the important part is to know that we have tried, really tried, to improve. Pluck up the courage to try this experiment, I can assure you that you will never regret it. Your life and many others can be changed for the better and they won't even know how it happened.

* * * * *

DISCONTENT

Let me tell you a story, an old story
Of things as they used to be.
Let me sing you a song, an old song
How people would like them to be.

There's a nostalgia abroad, loud and clear,
That tells of a hunger strong,
For days long ago, and not so long,
When people knew right from wrong.

The rat race is on, the winner goes on
To claim his brand new prize.
Another new car, a bright jazzy toy,
But what makes him heave a sigh?

A sigh for the days when life was lived,
And not just hurried through.
Yet people were just as busy then,
And troubles each fresh day brewed.

Has man ever paused, in his deadly rush
Like lemmings on to the sea.
To stop and wonder, deep and long,
What really the trouble could be.

That God in His wisdom, and seeing ahead
Made sure man was not satisfied.
Made him yearn to explore beyond the beyond
And new ways and means to try.

To try to find a meaning for life
Beyond the material world.
Until he learned, once and for all,
That his soul must be unfurled.

PROJECT

This project could be a very confronting one for many of you. It is to take a relationship that exists in your life – a BAD relationship – and begin to change it.

CHAPTER SIX

'The Real You'

Iwonder if you tried out the project I suggested or turned away from it. It is extremely important not to turn away from these situations because they come across your path in order that you may be given a chance to tackle them. They are not there by accident and must be solved sometime. Maybe I should say dissolved and the greatest dissolving solution is LOVE. It can act like water dripping gently on a stone. The very hardest situation can be worn away by just keeping on pouring love over it. Some people have said that they did not have a relationship of any kind that needed clearing up. What they did was to take a situation they did not like and try to clear that up. At the end of it all you must ask yourself. Did I fail or did I try?

THE RACE

And now the day is over
And the race is run,
You may sit down to rest,
My little one.

I do not need to know
That the way was hard,
But did you try, my son,
For that I'll take your word.

I know of the pain
And the loneliness too,
But throughout it all,
Did your smiles show through?

And who is this, my son,
Hanging on to your arm?
A friend you gave a lift to,
Helped save from harm.

You thought you'd lost the race,
As mankind you stopped to help.
But know this, little one –
The winner was yourself.

The Two Yous

Do you realise that there are two yous? They both have
very definite roles to play in life. If you do not agree with
me that the two do exist, try and do something that you
have been brought up to consider wrong. Why are you
hesitating?

Is there not a conversation going on inside yourself about
it? So, who does the other voice belong to? You may say:
"It is my conscience" It is a part of you, a part that belongs
to you and yet is different from another part of you.

Sometimes it does the prompting as to whether you will
do right or wrong (or at least it tries to). At other times it
can help in times of fear or danger. One part of you wants
to hold back, and at the same time there is another part of
you gently urging you to have courage. So just who are you
having the conversation with? Your other self.

Your other self can be quite a revelation to you if you
will but recognise it. It will give you help. Proper, practical,

logical help, not just airy-fairy imagination. It can guide you for your own good in all ways, not just the emotional way of the moment. It can give you words of wisdom when you need them, a sense of humour when it is essential, and a 'knowing' that there is a lot more of you yet to be discovered.

First of all you may be a little sceptical of all these profound statements. You have a right to be that way, until you prove it otherwise to your own satisfaction. Yet, until you try to prove it one way or the other, you will never know for sure what the real thing was.

If we now know for sure that we were created by God and not only that, but we are part of Him, isn't it time we stopped fearing Him more than loving Him? Many people think "I have been bad, or I am not good enough for God. Why should He bother with the likes of me?" If you are cold do you say, "I will warm myself before I go to the fire?" Do you not say, "I will go to the fire to warm myself?"

Let God Be The Judge

So it is with God. Let Him be the judge of how worthy you are. You are not capable of judging yourself fairly, one way or the other. When we do judge ourselves, it is often much too harshly. You are much, much greater than you have any idea of at this moment.

We could be likened to a dry, even parched, rock-hard field. Suddenly there is a heavy and hard downpour of rain. The field greedily tries to drink in the rain, but it is a physical impossibility for more than a little of it to soak in. A lot runs to waste. Still, *some* penetrates and in doing so the ground becomes more receptive so that the next time it rains knowledge, more sinks in.

Now, in the field, in seed form – are potential flowers, with beauty, fragrance and hope for people. When the field becomes watered enough, it reaches the seeds and they begin to grow. So from this combination of field (Self), rain (Spiritual Understanding) and sun (Spiritual Love) come the flowers of ability. These improve the look and feel of the field and thus improve the lives of others, for the seeds from the flowers will drift, even if the field itself is not always aware. They will drift and land and take seed in some other fields (Selves). So as we try to help ourselves, we begin to be able to help others.

God gave us brains to use and He gave us tongues with which to question. Why do we let fear stand in the way of our questioning? What do we fear? God's rejection if we dare to say that we do not go along with something the Church has interpreted? Or written in a Bible?

Someone once asked which was the best Bible to read? The answer is "The Bible that speaks to the *soul* of the person reading it." By the way, you might like also to try reading *The Aquarian Gospel Of Jesus The Christ*. I can assure you that it will be a unique experience for you. There are specific keys within the quoted sayings that have to do with 'self-awareness' and the opening of the channel – clarifying our contact with our inner Self, the God part of ourself.

"Why?" is not a blasphemy

There are other books also that will speak to your soul. There are also new and additional ideas. You are not blaspheming God just because you say "Why?" You are learning to discern and trying to grow. God respects such a person and will send answers.

When we are children we have to accept pat answers to our questions. God let us grow up and mature and become more thoughtful, in order to use the thoughts and questions that demand an answer. If you do dare to question, you will find answers that will affect the whole of the rest of your life and beyond!

The only guilt in us is if we shut ourselves off from God. He exists and is available, once we will acknowledge that fact. First of all to ourselves and then to others, that they too may 'seek and find'.

We can make 'knowing' God and our real Self as difficult or as easy as we like. We can try or we can dismiss the whole thing as rubbish. It is entirely up to us. That is our free will.

All that I have shared here with you has been offered to you with the hope that it will come to mean something to you. Yet all the words used and taught here do not mean a thing unless they are used. The lessons have to BE us and we have to BE them. You cannot be taught the truth by me. I can only speak to you of my experience of it. You then have to experience it for yourself in order for it to be YOUR truth.

The supreme truth is to be found at the heart of all phenomena as well as at the heart of man. Flowers, potatoes, birds, animals, typhoons and snowflakes.

People have been given spiritual understanding through all the ages. The qualifications needed to receive it? A genuine need or desire. No more and no less.

As far as the work of God is concerned – no one is too illiterate or bad or stupid to be a channel. You set the limitations, not God. Look for the good points about yourself. Everyone has them. Why decry them. If you want to think negative things about yourself, then the world is quite happy to go along with that. They are equally busy thinking negative thoughts about themselves. So what happens when you try the positive aspects. Thought is the most powerful thing there is. By its use we can change our world. Notice that point – not just by the thinking but by its USE. Find the real you, make friends with it and let it help you.

* * * * *

PROJECT

To sit down and ask God if you can be a co-worker with Him (not for Him, but with Him).

CHAPTER SEVEN

Alive or Just Living?

Many people spend their whole lives waiting for the next thing to happen to them. Much of the time this next happening will hopefully produce that perfect happiness, be it a new job, a new home or a new friend. So often they wait and wait, often in vain.

Each day is one of the keys to our happiness. Each day has its own importance. Each day can have its own movement, its own growth. Even negative things can be growth if you are prepared to try and search out their hidden lessons.

So – what importance does 'Each Day' have to you? Whether you live with family, friends or alone, I ask you again – What importance does each day have to you? Are you alive or just living?

What might I mean by that question? Of course you are alive – you are breathing aren't you? You know you exist. You have a physical body that feels pain if you injure it. You have a brain that thinks out answers to problems. You have a part that you call your emotions that can be moved to laughter or tears or anger. So you are a complete person. Physically, Mentally and Emotionally. All of these parts function fairly well and allow you to give expression to yourself as a human being. BUT – are you just a human being?

Or is there something more to you? Is there a need for you to become aware, really aware, that there is much more to you than just being a human being and much more to 'Being Alive' than 'Just Living'.

Most people's lives are lived in a morass of habits. There is nothing necessarily bad about this. Certain habits are essential to us in order to get through our daily lives. However, what has happened to the masses is that they have come to regard habits as the essence of life – as all there is or all there can be.

It is a fact that to be really 'Alive' you have to become what I call 'Aware' people. An 'Aware' person is someone who has the need or the courage to ask questions of life. Almost to be greedy for an experience of living beyond the normal, mundane things of life.

What right do you have to expect more, almost to demand more? How many times in your life have you said *The Lord's Prayer*? Think of what you have said time and time again. How does it begin? OUR FATHER ... How many of you have ever thought about claiming your right – your heritage?

The fact that you really are a child of God. That you have within you – even if in seed form as yet – a perfected part of you that can grow daily if only you will nurture and believe in it.

So, can you begin to prove this theory of becoming 'Alive' even whilst you are still 'Living'? It is, in fact, very very important to be able to prove to your own satisfaction that this seemingly nebulous idea of a different *quality* of life can be experienced here and now.

The first thing is to sit quietly at regular intervals and imagine who you really are. You are a child of God. What can that mean? Imagine the power, wisdom and love that is locked up inside you. Feel and sense the great light that is you. Even if you feel that you are play-acting to begin with, do it anyway. It is another name for Faith.

Don't worry about how evolved or wise or clever or spiritual you think you are, or are not, right now. It is almost impossible for you to see with any degree of honesty what level of understanding you are really at, and human nature, being what it is, usually guides you to put yourself down harder than the Heavenly Father ever does. So accept that you *are* all right. Just the fact that you are trying to grow, turning your face towards your real Home is cause for much rejoicing in the higher spheres.

Now, how about other people. Will they notice anything? Yes! They will sense this 'Coming to life' that is going on with you. They will sense a light, an alertness, a 'something' that was not there before. (In actual fact it was already there before, but you had amnesia.) It will make them ask you, often with puzzlement in their voices: "What do you believe in?" or "I want to know what you know", or "You seem to have something – what is it?" or even "Can I talk to you?"

Let me give you a very important point right now, at this very point in time. When it happened to me, often from complete strangers I very quickly learned to say inwardly "Can I please have the right words?" and you will be amazed and very humble at what help will be given to you. Please do not feel that you are not qualified to answer their questions. Whatever they need to know or hear at this point in time will be exactly what you will find you have the ability to do. You *will* give then good answers and surprise yourself as you maybe hear yourself telling them something you don't recall having read about or heard about before. Just try it all out for yourself. Don't be afraid to practise. After all, everything you have ever accomplished in life so far took practice didn't it? So take time and practise (practise means repeating something regularly) trying out the art of being 'Alive and Aware' not 'Just Alive'.

Although you have been shown the availability of a greater awareness, it might have crossed your mind to wonder how you get from the point of questioning to the point of proving?

There is a bridge. Of what does the bridge consist? What are its ingredients?

1. The first ingredient needed is the energy or incentive to mentally create the bridge. It can, in fact, be of any texture you choose. Stone, wood, marble, reed, a rainbow bridge. (Use your imagination.)

2. The next ingredient is the wisdom to believe in the availability of the bridge.

3. Another ingredient is love. Love for yourself, for the inner permanent real part of yourself. Love enough for yourself that says you deserve more – more understanding and experiencing of who you really are. A child of God.

4. Another really important ingredient is Faith. The faith that a contact really is possible. This ingredient could be the most important one of the lot. Faith strong enough to 'Know' there is a Father who truly loves you, faith that He will come more than halfway over the bridge to meet you (Are you not a dearly loved Prodigal Son?) and faith that He waits and waits so patiently for you to take that first step upon the bridge, the bridge of understanding who you *really* are. A special child of God. Unique, individual and needed by God as much as you need Him. Why not give it a try?

PROJECT

Take one aspect of your life that you don't like. Look at it without emotion, study it, think about it and then come up with three possible solutions.

CHAPTER EIGHT

Death and Suicide

Why write about death and suicide when happiness is what the world is striving for? Before I go any further maybe you would like to take a few moments and sit and think as to what your concept of happiness is? Have you had some time or times in your life when you were perfectly happy? What were they like? Were you by yourself when they happened? Was just one other person involved? Did you have to struggle to achieve this happiness or did it just happen to you? Last of all, could you contain this happiness and do you have it now? Can you guarantee that you will always be able to find it and have it just when you want it? On what does it depend? If happiness is a tangible thing that we can grasp at, why would *anyone* want to commit suicide.

I once gave a class and all I took were the two words 'Death and Suicide'. The strange thing was that I attracted no less than three strangers to that class that particular night, all of whom had tried to commit suicide in the past. They all agreed that although they went through the motions of trying to kill themselves, deep down they did not think they would end up dead. What they needed from this action was to be noticed or to try and make someone feel guilty for certain actions towards them, or to hopefully obtain a love that was being denied them. These three were lucky. They lived to learn to live another day. I have bad contact with someone who was not so lucky. He succeeded!

The incident took place when I was living in America for a while with a friend of a friend. I did not know Kathy before I went to live with her, although we found that we got along famously. However, not too long after I had moved in, as I was meditating in the early hours of one morning, I became aware that Kathy's dead son Michael was with me. I did not know what he looked like and still do not know, but I just knew it was Michael. What he found now that he was in the spirit world, was that he was held near the earth plane by his mother's guilt that she had contributed seriously to his committing suicide. What followed over the next few months would take too long to tell, but it took much time and patience on all our parts to finally sort out the facts and release all the negativities and guilt. If only those who contemplate suicide would or could realise that far from death being an end to their troubles, they are just the beginning of a new and more serious kind.

Whether one knows it or not, we all asked to come back here for a chance to work out some of our soul growth. There is a shortage of vehicles (baby bodies) and it really is a sin to take on a body, and then, if things get tough, to opt out early. Maybe, when the going gets really rough, that is the time to let go and really ask for help from the only One who is available at any time of the day or night. We just have to ask and have faith that there will be an answer.

Sometimes people commit suicide in another way. They commit suicide to life, to challenges, to relationships. Instead of living they are already dead, although they are still breathing. I remember reading about a girl who, in her early twenties, had an accident and was paralysed from the neck downwards. For a long time she struggled to come to terms with it and then one day it dawned on her that, except for the fact that she could not clean her teeth for herself etc., she was not so different from thousands of other people who lived their lives like zombies, doing the same thing every day, over and over again, the same thing every weekend, thinking the same thoughts and watching the same TV programmes. Living through other people's experiences and gathering none for themselves.

I do realise that for many of you, there is no choice but to live life on a very regular and seemingly mundane level.

There are family responsibilities that make it impossible to go out and have adventures, even if we do feel as if we are pioneers deep down. So what can we explore? How can we have adventures? Where can we go within the framework of our life to grow through experience? Why should we feel the need to grow anyway?

Spiritual Growth

Because man is basically creative and because man, somewhere inside KNOWS that he is immortal. So, why do we fear death? Because it seems unknown to us. Yet there are on record nowadays, some excellent accounts of people who have died for a space of time and returned to tell what they experienced. Some say it is all imagination. Well, I always think that even imagination must have a reality.

One of the best areas where we can bring together a lot of the questions I have been tossing out at you, is in our spiritual growth. There you can have adventures, be pioneers and learn that death is just a transition from one body to another and from one phase of ongoing existence to another. It is something to be looked forward to, not feared. However, that does not mean that we should just sit down and wait for the day of death to come. If you were going to climb a mountain, wouldn't you enjoy it much more if you learned about and practiced climbing some smaller mountains or hills. If you made yourself physically fit so that it was a pleasure and not a penance.

Without spiritual growth we cannot go far, and without working at our spiritual growth, bit by bit the growth will be nil. If you buy a plant and leave it on the shelf long enough without any attention, it will die. If you buy timber to make a chair and leave it on the shelf long enough, it will rot away. If you buy a 'Do-it-Yourself' book on learning a language and do not study it regularly and practice it, then the language will never be learned.

Slowly, our spiritual understanding will grow – if we keep trying with it. If we believe in God, then we need to acknowledge Him. If we believe that Jesus lived, then what did he live for? If we believe that he lived to teach us something, then what are we doing about learning, understanding and putting the teachings in to practice. That is the only way we can prove or disprove their validity. (The *Aquarian Gospel Of Jesus The Christ* is a very, very nice book!)

Right now, you are here on earth. Whether you like it very much or not, you ARE here. It is hard to believe that things will ever be any different to what they are now. We sometimes take it for granted that nothing will change. That if times are bad they will always bad. That we have plenty of time to put right things that are wrong.

Our bodies

Our thoughts

Our way of living

Our relationships

Yet, how much time do we really have? Nothing can be guaranteed but this moment in time. Yesterday has gone for ever and simply cannot be recalled. But we do have today. We also have forever, but the very quality of our existence at any given time, depends upon the use we make of our talents, however humble. Our free will to experience more, even as we go about our daily tasks. If we do not use these talents, this free will, then it can be as if we are already dead. Life is for the living.

* * * * *

SUICIDE

The evening had come – I was all alone,
For you had gone your way.
I had no one to worry – no one to care,
And I couldn't find God to pray.

We'd been happy those days – alone in our world,
With no thought for other folk.
Then came the quarrels – with shouts loud and clear –
The comments no longer a joke.

As I sat in the twilight and realised the truth
That you did no longer care,
I felt that my sorrow – expressed in my tears –
I could no longer bear.

Now the tablets sat on the table near
A large bottle for to see.
I'd show her what she'd done this day,
I'd make her sorry for me.

I sat and mused before the final step,
And I felt I began to dream.
An angel stood with tears in his eyes
Speaking to me, it would seem.

'God gave you this life – with love in His heart
And you gladly accepted the tasks.
Would you throw His gift in His face today?
Tear a piece of Him apart?'

True, the lover has gone you gave your love to,
And the world seems a lonely place,
But if only you look around you each day,
There are others to take her place.

So think of the love you still have to give,
Of the lonely ones waiting for you,
If you die by your hand – this very day,
Your troubles just start anew.

As he finished speaking in a quiet solemn voice,
He started fading away.
But I knew he had saved my soul right then,
Death must wait on another day!

* * * * *

PROJECT

Study this chapter slowly and in silence. See if you can open yourself up to new understandings of Life and Death in a positive way.

CHAPTER NINE

Forgiveness – Why Forgive?

O n reading through this last chapter, I felt that maybe I should expand a little more on the area of suicide and what I found out through my contact with Michael on the other side, plus some direct channelling when asked a question at one of my classes as to my understanding of suicides.

I was given the understanding that anyone who commits suicide has to accept the responsibility not only for this action to themselves, but for the various and often very, very strong reactions from those that are left behind.

In Michael's case he was only seventeen and had gone to live with Kathy (M's mother) when she remarried. There was some jealousy on his part about the new stepfather and it came to a head one day when Michael wanted his mother to help him with some studying and she did not want to. In a fit of temper he went out into the garage and hanged himself.

He told me from the spirit world that he had not meant to take it to its ultimate, but that he was so annoyed with her because she did not seem to care enough about him, now that she had a new husband. He did regret his action, but the price that he now had to pay was that he could go nowhere and do nothing until the guilt that Kathy felt about the incident had bees lifted. That was not an easy task. Apart from a letter about all this that he dictated to me, he eventually came to us one Sunday afternoon as we were sitting in front of the fire, and we did have a three way conversation, with many tears from Kathy.

Michael wanted her to get rid of his clothes, books, records etc. that she was clinging on to and wanted to keep as mementoes. Eventually the anniversary of his death arrived and Kathy was really distraught. Michael came to me and begged me to talk with his mother. It was not an easy thing to do as she was deep in her guilt and grief, but his words to her were that if she loved him she would let the guilt go and so release him.

Finally she did so as I was standing in front of her and the cloud around her physically lifted. Later that year she told me that she had sensed Michael around her. Now the guilt was gone and the love alone remained, although she would always miss him.

The Need To Grow

Whether he knows it or not, one of the greatest needs man has is the need to grow. To grow physically in health, mentally in alertness (and age is no excuse), emotionally in stability and spiritually in understanding. To grow in any or all of these areas you must have energy. The energy to pull yourself away from the inertia of laziness. The energy to use your brain in thinking more and in finding things to concentrate on. The energy to overcome depression or fits of anger. Maybe the most important is the energy to search for a deeper meaning to life – a spiritual search that can colour your everyday life with a different meaning.

So, what has growth got to do with forgiveness? By not being forgiving you are the one who is suffering, even more than the one who you need to forgive. Feelings of unforgiveness are actual blocks, solid blocks of negative energy held within yourself and blocking your creativity. Energy, in order to be beneficial HAS to flow. If it is blocked by negative energy of any kind, there will be an unease within you, even though you may not be consciously aware of it.

Maybe someone HAS done you a great wrong and you do not feel justified in forgiving. It would look to you like weakness, as though you condoned the wrong or even agreed with it? Several things need to be carefully checked out at this point. How do you feel, really feel, as you think of the misunderstanding? Do you feel a sense of power over the other person? Do you feel a sadness at a relationship that was and is no longer? Or do you still feel hurt and angry at how little they thought of you to do such a thing? Then how about pride? I know someone who was quite proud, it seemed to me, to say "I can forgive, but I cannot forget". Unless you can eventually forget, or pour such love over the condition that exists so as to make the feelings dilute to nothing, then you have not truly forgiven.

Cause and Effect

There is a natural law, the law of Karma, otherwise called the Law of Cause and Effect, that balances out our lives perfectly. Whether we believe in it or not is quite immaterial. An agreement to that law is even written into the Lord's Prayer 'Forgive us our trespasses as we forgive those that trespass against us.' Jesus added even more to it when Peter asked him how many times we should forgive. Do *you* remember the answer? Seven times seventy! Yet how many of us refuse to forgive even once? Yet your unforgiveness festers inside you like a sore. It never really heals.

This fact also applies to the wrongs you yourself have committed over the years. Not only to others, but to yourself. Guilt is part of that sore and it can actually make you ill both mentally and physically, The healing ointment for all these ailments and grievances is forgiveness and the bandage to hold the ointment on with is LOVE.

As for yourself – you special, unique, individual, dearly loved child of God – you are trying to grow up – so why expect yourself to be adult and perfect all at once. How can you really forgive, love and care for others in a natural way if you don't even forgive, love and care for yourself!

If we have done wrong, either intentionally, or unintentionally and now we feel the need to punish ourselves, think carefully. If we said a harsh word out of place, or forgot to send a letter, or a card or telephone someone, then let the atonement be that we forgive others their frailties. There is always a lesson to be learned from someone who has hurt you, in whatever form. At the same time, the ever present law of Cause and Effect will always take care of whatever judging is necessary. There is no way that we can know all the circumstances that caused the hurt to take place and so our judgment would always be faulty. Once again Jesus mentioned this:

'Pass no judgement and you will not be judged. For as you judge others, so you will yourselves be judged, and whatever measure you deal out to others will be dealt back to you.' (Matthew 7:1 and 2)

FORGIVENESS

As he walked down the street towards me today,
My face quickly turned the other way.
I hated him for seeming so bold,
For showing a smile and not being cold.

He had wronged me that day when we stood and talked,
Had shown me some truths and nothing had shirked.
I couldn't forgive the things he had said,
Yet the back of my mind lurked some things I had read.

"Forgive them Lord, they know not what they do."
Was it now my turn these things to try and prove?
If someone could forgive so much pain and punishment,
Should I make such a fuss about my meagre treatment?

So I slowly turned my head and with an effort gave a nod,
Tears started in his eyes and he quickly crossed the road.
"Forgive me my friend for my thoughtless words,
        that hurt you deeply, I know."
So I tried, I forgave, and in the end,
        we have only love to show.

* * * * *

PROJECT

Take a big leap forward spiritually and see if you can practice forgiveness in even one area of your life that might need it.

CHAPTER TEN

Sowing and Growing. What?

To go back a little on the subject of Forgiveness. Let us take a hypothetical case of John wronging you – of robbing you of a job that you knew was yours by right – a promotion that you felt that you deserved and also financially needed. You cannot forgive him for taking your opportunity. Yet may he not have done you a favour in disguise? It all depends on how you cope with it. If you sit and feel hatred for him and sorrow for yourself then you sit with those heavy lumps of inertia within yourself. But what if you release it, give an inner blessing to his success with the job and see if maybe you can stretch your energy out in other directions.

May it not be a higher wisdom than yours that can see what you really need in order to grow and learn in life. So two forgivenesses here could make a brand new life.

(1) Forgive him for doing what seemed to be a wrong.

(2) Forgive yourself for a seeming failure and see what direction, what new direction, you should flow in. That released energy could thoroughly surprise you.

I fully realise that it is one thing to read or hear about what an act of forgiveness will do, and it is quite another thing to try and do it. That is the hardest part. You have to want to do it. It takes great moral courage to say and mean "I forgive you" then by letting it all go and forgetting too. But what have you to lose except a big chunk of negative energy and a surprising good feeling creeping in.

Sowing Seeds

A man knocked at a door one hot summer's day and asked if he could have a drink of water. The owner said that if he would wait on the bench under the shade of the tree he would bring him a glass of lemonade. Years later the owner went to Egypt to explore the desert for ancient ruins. One day, by accident he wandered from his friends and eventually found himself lost – with no water. AS he staggered on, he knew that if he did not find water soon he was done for.

Suddenly he saw a small group of palm trees which indicated water. He knew that it might be a mirage, but as be got nearer he could see the glint of the sun on the water and hear the beautiful music of a gentle trickle as the small pond was fed. He drank his fill and soaked his clothes and waited in the shade of the trees until nightfall when he heard shouts and saw lights.

Within twenty minutes he had walked in the direction of his friends who were out looking for him. When they got back to camp he recounted his experience and was startled to hear the guides say "There is no oasis for at least ten miles around here!"

TITHING – What?

We get what we give, so the story goes,
But who can convince, who really knows?
A little bit of fear, at this stage intervenes,
Maybe we need to give, to materialise our dreams.

So what shall we give, we generously cry,
"I'll think about it, in a while, by and by."
"And don't forget," you may proudly say,
"I gave some money in church today."

So the days go by, and the weeks and the years,
"Tomorrow I'll give, have no fears."
Now the years have formed a lifetime for you,
In death you go forward, for the angel to view.

"Tell me about it, your life and your deeds,
How much effort did you make, to plant God's seeds?"
I stuttered and stumbled, began to blink,
"Wait a minute, don't rush me, just let me think."

"A man on the street, had a flag to sell,
I gave him a coin, didn't I do well?"
"Don't ask me," said the Angel with a smile,
Just sit yourself down and think for a while.

* * * * *

Tithing is the same as sowing – it grows. Old debts are paid back, be they good or bad. It is up to you just what you sow. I grew up believing that if you gave 10% of your earnings to the church, you were assured of a place in heaven. It was your passport and beyond that you did not have to worry a great deal. The original idea was that the church could not be a proper business and earn its own profits therefore it had to rely on the 10% from the people. I want to propose a new idea to you. Try tithing other things as well, not just money. For example, try tithing 10% of your time. Write a letter to someone who would love to hear from you, make that long overdue phone call. Tithe some extra time on yourself, in improving yourself.

Sowing and Reaping

If we still accept the principle that it is good to tithe, then set about proving to yourself that it really is a valid thing to do. Time is the raw stuff that tithing is made of. How we tithe our time can bring us increased profit of health and money and more. Watch for the results. Do you secretly think that God prefers you unhealthy and poor? You are one of His children and maybe the hardest thing is for us to accept that honour.

If you are healthy you feel good and this reflects outwards and other people benefit. If you earn good money, you can flow that out in all sorts of way, so that once again you benefit, even as you try to benefit others.

So how can you achieve more each day? See quite clearly what it is that fills up the day. How much is repetitious and time wasting? Do you always have to read the newspaper and watch every news on the TV? So much of the news is negative, that it can pull us down. We need to find things that lift us up. Goals, realistic goals are one answer.

Everyone, no matter what your status in life, has the ability to set some little goal to improve things. You just have to want it. All of this is rather on the surface level. Let us look at tithing in a deeper sense.

Whether you believe it or not, you get back in life in direct proportion to what you expect or what you feel you deserve. This means in *all* areas of your life. If you have, as yet, no experience of God, that does not mean that God does not exist. It only means that God does not exist for you yet. If I go days at a time without meditating (prayer is you talking TO God and meditating is you listening FOR God) then how can I expect to have any relationship with God?

What is a real relationship? It is communication. Communication with God IS possible. All you have to do is to prove it for yourself. In that way only will you 'know', rather than just understand.

You are a part of God, a child of God, a great spiritual being here on earth in seed form. You were put on earth in order that you might grow, Your roots have to cling firmly to the earth with all its problems and troubles. Your shoots will turn upward to the 'inner light'. Try and sit quietly each day and 'feel' the spiritual rain that will surround you with peace and comfort. Why should you have faith? Why not?

Take a lettuce seed. Cut it open (if you can.) Where is the lettuce? Take a tulip bulb. Just one. Cut it in half from top to bottom. Where is the flower, the colour, the perfume and the leaves? If you want to have the potential of these things proved to you, you will never get the lettuce or the flower. You plant them with trust. God provides the miracle. Plant yourself down at least once each day regularly and find that circle of silence that is in your heat. Go into it and wait. As the lettuce does not appear overnight or the bulb flower immediately, so you, too, must have patience. God knows what you are about and this tithing of time will, above all, bear fruits more satisfying than any other.

I feel the power so strongly around me that I know enough is written for now. Spend time trying out this idea. Tithing time to God is so very important and I must restate: "All that you sow, must grow and will be returned to you, with profit."

* * * * *

IS IT TIME TO SIT AND LISTEN

In the days long ago, when the world was young,
We all sang together our Father's song.
Now aeons have passed, we have played our games
Of hate and war and greedy things.

We play harder and harder, all the sexy games –
What different and new can we do?
Maybe love and fulfilment the old fashioned way,
Would refresh and content us anew.

Some folk are around who begin to mistrust,
And are turning aside to the quieter lanes.
Too much loud living, noise and fuss,
Is there joy and peace on different planes?

A peace that will rest midst a raging store,
A contentment that feeds the inner longing,
Finds love in a glance of all passion shorn,
And sits and listens for God's Special Song.

The Song that says who you really are,
And what you will one day be,
The Song that angels sing from afar,
That echoes to Eternity.

PROJECT

What little seed might you sow right now? Of love, or caring, or physical improvement, or a new learning idea or some spiritual trust, faith and growth?

CHAPTER ELEVEN

Healing, Self-Healing too?

If someone talks about healing, we automatically think of an injured body being put to rights. Yet the mind is an integral part of the body. If the mind is injured, not necessarily physically, but by words or actions of another, then it too can be said to be ill or sick. Our emotions are often in a bad way. Hate, envy, anger can all affect us as deeply as any bodily illness and all may need a healing power.

Everything we do or say was a thought first, so in some way our physical, mental and emotional sufferings have originated from our own thoughts or thought reaction to others. Sometimes people talk in a negative way about other people, but many more times they think negatively about themselves. How many of us like the way we look? Even a beautiful woman or a handsome man has been heard to decry a face that is getting lined and older looking. Another thing is that many of us harbour very strong guilt feelings because we did this thing and we didn't do that thing. Because we do not feel that we are perfect, we tend to lose sight of all the good that we do have within us that shows already to people.

It has been proved that sick people with a positive attitude will heal faster than people with a negative attitude. Years ago I regularly got colds (and the sympathy that went with them?) One day I decided that I was not going to get colds anymore no matter how many people sneezed their germs over me. That was many years ago and in all that time I have had two occasions when I had what I chose to call 'A Cleansing'. That lasted no more than one day each time. Coincidence? Maybe, but I choose to call it power of mind over matter. In case I sound too goody-goody two shoes, recently I did have a cold, cough and chest that lasted for well over a week. Maybe I had been boasting too much?

There is a particular passage in the *Aquarian Gospel Of Jesus The Christ from* Chapter 91 Verses 8-17 that is so apt that I would like to share it with you:

And Jesus said to him, "My brother man, would you be healed?" The man replied, "I earnestly desire to be healed, but am helpless and when the angel comes and pours the healing virtues in the pool, another who can walk steps in the fountain first and I am left unhealed" And Jesus said, "Who sends an angel here to potentise (endow with energy) this pool just for a favoured few? I know it is not God for he deals just the same with everyone. One has no better chance in heaven's healing fountain than another one. The fount of health is in your soul, it has a door locked fast, the key is faith, and everyone can have this key and may unlock the door and plunge into the healing fount and be made whole."

And then the man looked up in hopeful mood and said, "Give me this key of faith." And Jesus said, "Do you believe what I have said? According to your faith it shall be done. Arise, take up your bed and walk." Jesus went on to talk further with the now healed man and told him to sin no more.

This story suggests to me that we often punish ourselves and keep ourselves unwell because we feel guilty about something, even though it may be on a subconscious level. This is the acting out of the law of Karma, otherwise called the law of Cause and Effect. Sickness of any kind is for a reason. Either the paying of a debt or the learning of a necessary lesson. Many people, when they first learn about this law, get very depressed, because they cannot remember what they have done to earn their sickness. However, although *you* may not remember, your Soul knows what it is all about and why it is happening. That is the level where most of the learning goes on.

The Law of Grace

The positive side to all of this is that there exists another law: The Law of Grace. This law can supersede or override the Law of Karma and cause a healing to take place. Try to accept the lesson the disability is trying to teach you, have faith that you no longer need it and let it go. If you notice, time and time again Jesus said, "Thy faith hath made thee whole" He did not say that he had made them whole. So, true healing is not only that the afflicted person has faith in the healer, but he has faith that he deserves to be healed. Let the faith well up from that deep inner well of your being.

As you carry out these suggestions, two things will happen. One is that by the faith self-healing can take place, but we will also notice that people are put across our path that need some healing energy from you. Physically by a touch, mentally by a kind word and emotionally by a smile. Just have the confidence to allow yourself to become a channel. Each one of us can affect so many people in so many ways. Sometimes we are not even aware of the affect we have had.

I was on a beach in America once and stopped to talk for a few moments to a young girl I had seen at a local seminar. To my knowledge we chatted for about three or four moments about nothing in particular. I did happen to mention that I travelled quite a bit and she said how lucky I was. I replied that I had found out that wherever *you* travel you take yourself with you. A week later, just as she was leaving to go home, she came to me with a little gift and tears in her eyes. She said that she had been going to run away from school and home (age 18) as she did not like either. My words had made her look at the situation again and she finally realised that a lot of the problem stemmed from herself. So, you can see how God uses us if we will let Him. That girl went back home and finished her education. Just a 'chance meeting'?

So much still to say, to share and learn. Yet, of all these lessons surely the greatest is still this from the *Aquarian Gospel of Jesus The Christ*, page 51.

And Jesus said, "I do not see a greatest of the Ten Commands. I see a golden cord that runs through all the Ten Commands that binds them fast and makes them one. This cord is love and it belongs to every word of all the Ten Commands. If one is full of love he can do nothing else than worship God, for God is love."

He goes on to say that: "love is strong enough to open any human door so the truth can enter in and cause the heart to understand" Are you going to open up your heart?

HEALER?

Jesus taught lessons a long time ago,
Yet his words are fresh with truth.
'These things I achieve, not only me,
But you can do them to.'

I pondered and wondered for many a day
Why we seemed so far behind.
Why we seemingly are so ignorant still,
And seemingly spiritually blind.

A few people there are who lay on hands,
And miracles seem to appear.
But what of the rest of us, you and me,
Why are our lives so bare?

Now I hear the postman at the door,
A letter there for me.
It looked quite innocent lying there,
Yet its contents set me free.

A friend that I met with a week ago,
Wrote to tell me how she felt.
The chat we had, the quick cup of tea,
Had relieved her of her guilt.

So let us remember when we say our prayers
To ask for the chances to heal.
A miracle touch, a miracle word,
Let God the opportunities reveal.

* * * * *

PROJECT

How about practising the following affirmation for ten minutes each day, whilst looking at yourself in the mirror. You might be pleasantly surprised at the results!!

DAILY AFFIRMATION FOR THE SUBCONSCIOUS
(To be spoken out loud)

I am whole, I am perfect,
I am healthy, I am strong,
I am calm, I am loving,
I am happy, I am successful.

* * * * *

If you have trouble weight-wise, this is a nice addition.
I eat when I am hungry, with concentration.
I stop when I am satisfied.

* * * * *

CHAPTER TWELVE –

Love. Lovable Me?

As a child I did not think I was lovable. I could not reason this out completely, but certainly my poor little face came in for a lot of research. My chin was a funny shape, my hair too thick and straight and my nose too snub. When I was ten I even wrote it in an essay – that I was not lovable because my nose was too snub. How many of you have been there? How many of you do not like yourselves, let alone love yourself. Yet we do need to know that we are lovable. Why do we have this need? It is simply this. In order to have satisfying relationships with others, we have to, first of all, have a satisfying relationship with ourselves. This can be one of the hardest and most challenging things to bring about. Wise men have said: "Know thyself." Maybe they should have added: "But be kind to yourself – as you would to a helpless child."

If you have any belief at all in a God, then have belief that He is a loving God. He loves without strings. Do you? Do you say to yourself that you will like yourself when you are slim, or when you give up drinking or when other people appear to like you? What has to happen is that you begin with love.

You are a true child of God and have a pure perfect core. All the rest is just dross that has collected around you. Ask God for unconditional love to be poured over you and feel the dross melt away. Don't try all by yourself to become perfect and think that then you will be acceptable to God, Go inwardly just as you are and see how you are met more than half way. Try it. Do it! Do not just read this and forget it. Live it and experience it – for yourself.

The tremendous possibility of feasting upon each day as it comes, moment by moment, slips past us and we are left searching for the rainbow.

God is made up of three parts:

The Father   –   Power or Force
The Mother   –   Wisdom
The Son   –   Love

BELOVED

To know you are loved – even when you are old,
Is to know there is someone who cares.
To know you are numbered where angels unfold,
And the stars wink away their tears.

To know you are lovable – whilst wearing a frown
And important to someone inside,
Is to know you are child of 'I am that I am',
And that nothing really dies.

To know you are God to some little cell,
Who tries to follow your whim,
Is to know that nameless unknown Cause
That sits without – yet within.

To know you are cell of a heavenly host
Who need your loving care,
Is to find joy in this life in everything,
And no cross too hard to bear.

You can flicker – grow dim – but not go out,
You child of all that is.
So grow to the stature that beckons and calls,
And 'know' what life is about.

* * * * *

Love

Love – we set the rules for our love. Most of the time
the rule is that we wish to receive love more than to give
it. If we do give it, there are often conditions that the other
person, child or animal, should behave in a certain way. A
child should know that it is loved in spite of its wrongdoings.
A marriage breakdown. When we are first in the company
of the loved one we accept them as they are. Then we begin
to give the love with rules attached. We intimate that we
will only love if we are obeyed in certain things or treated
in certain ways. Suddenly we don't like the hairstyle or the
earrings or the sniffling. Many partners in the end do not
even know any longer that they are still loved because it is
smothered in the sauce of disapproval. So practice giving
love in spite of the imperfections that you see, which are but
reflections of yourself.

Remember that before you can really love anyone else,
you must love yourself. Real love is like white light. It has
within it a range of colours, feeling and emotions. Very rarely
is our love pure. Even if you just practice liking yourself, it
is a step in the right direction.

To love oneself is not to give in to all feelings and needs
and wants that cross our path. A child who is happiest is
one who is fairly disciplined. A dog is most content when it
knows where it stands with its master. So our physical self

needs to know how far it can go in self-indulgence. It also needs to know where the self-indulgence stops and the self-discipline starts. But self-discipline tempered by love and respect for our bodies will not create stress in the same way as if we hate ourselves for what we are.

Today is a fresh today and we do not have to be in the same spot that we were yesterday. You have free will to change things. Make this life an adventure INWARDLY, even if you cannot adventure outwardly. Nothing need be static. To be static is to be dead before you are dead.

LOVE

This I would have, a room on my own,
Where I could communicate with Mother, Father in One.
But life is so busy, the house is so full,
Where is the space my wishes to fulfil?

The room I am in contains me and another,
Not the spirit of God, but my noisy brother.
I said to myself, "He is not like me,
Always kidding and joking, no sense of reverie."

Musing these ideas into the garden I wandered
To perceive my brother under the apple tree yonder.
What was he doing with his form so still?
The shine on his face gave me a thrill.

As he opened his eyes, the usual grin appeared
"Why the bewilderment, do you think I am weird?
Don't you know that for me, my day is not complete,
Unless I sit in quiet and with my Maker communicate."

We are brothers, dear brother, beyond our normal life;
Come, let us share the silence with a double prayer tonight.
For did not Jesus say, all those many years ago,
That where two or three are gathered, there will I be too?

* * * * *

PROJECT

Love. Even plants are susceptible to love. You can make your garden GLOW. Even if there is someone you know almost hates you, if you silently send them love energy EVERY DAY, in time it will dissolve the hate away. It has been proved.

CHAPTER THIRTEEN

Loneliness

For many people Earth is all there is. It is a place where they have been born, with no choice as to where or when. Their only hope in life is that when the day comes to die, they will have managed to earn a good enough grade to go to a nebulous Heaven with streets of gold, and nothing to do but sing hymns.

But some of you have learned differently. Some of you march to a different tune from the rest of the world. Sometimes this 'knowing', this 'understanding' causes you pain. You feel alien, misunderstood, even lonely, even when you are with other people. You are hungry for contact with kindred souls and they seem hard to find. Sometimes you wish that you could forget what you have discovered, because it causes you moments of guilt, moments of discomfort. Try as you may – you no longer fit with the masses. You are different. You 'know'!

Knowing

But some of you may still be wondering: "What is the 'knowing' that is written about?" It is a knowing, first by hope and faith, then by intuition, that Earth and its inhabitants are not just dumped here, inwardly alone and outwardly often stressed. There is more to life, much more.

Just ask questions – at this stage – of yourself. Don't be afraid to question – even God. You were given a brain and intelligence to use. You do not have to be intellectual, just brave enough to question and question and question. Once God (or whatever or whoever you think runs the Universe) sees that you are sincere and persistent with your questions you WILL be given answers. I ask you to at least have faith in the idea, because it is so. I did it and proved it to myself.

So many times we set God apart, or block God out. Sometimes it is because of fear (fear that God is displeased with us), or sometimes it is because of guilt (that we have not done the things we know we should have done.) Whether we know it or not, understand it or not, we are all God's children. The reason we are lonely is that we have shut ourselves away from our real Family and our real Home.

Don't try to be perfect before you approach God. That again is like trying to get warm before you approach the fire. Do it. You will be very pleasantly surprised at the results.

EARTH'S REALITY

For some on Earth, the life seems hard,
Not just in the ways of work,
There's a loneliness, a kind of ache,
For things we cannot shirk.

We seem to have freedom to come and go,
And sip at life's rich fare.
Yet underneath we ponder on
Is it freedom or really a snare?

Why do some of our plans get kicked away,
And tossed in a heap on the side?
Why do some of the folk we care about
Turn away, even though we cry?

If we think on the surface and only that way,
Then life will return the act.
For life wears a mask – a sweet façade,
Quite different when seen from the back.

Some people I know – just a few,
Have seen through this sweet charade.
They are asking questions loud and clear,
And the answers are there to be heard.

Enjoy life to the full – sip deep and long –
No one will stand in your way.
But remember the cost – payment in full
Will be demanded one day.

So balance all things, the outer and inner,
For each has their part to play.
You are no more a puppet or sinner,
If you conduct your life this way.

THE LONELY SOUL

There was once a Soul. It had been created by a Great
Being with Shiny Eyes, called God. It was made of pure love
and light and it enjoyed its existence with every particle of its
being. It played with its Soul Mates near to its Father/Mother
house each day. It experimented with the gifts its Parents
had given it, such as conducting the flowers into wonderful
orchestrations of music, colour and perfume, all combined.

It had Wisdom for breakfast. Laughter for Lunch and Love
for Supper. At night it rested at peace near to its Mother/
Father Being; their hearts gently beating in unison.

Eventually however, the Soul began to get adventuresome and to stray further and further from the House each day. It began to get bolder with its experiments with the trees and flowers and to create discords within their orchestrations and to laugh at the flowers' discomfort. When another Soul remonstrated with it, it pushed its brother/sister away and so created further disturbances, especially as other Souls began to imitate it.

One night, after having quite a grand day of causing chaos and confusion, it felt that it could not be bothered to go Home, so it stayed out. The following day it felt even more adventuresome and so wandered further away still. Its experiments with its power became even more daring and as time passed many of its brother/sister Soul beings heard of its adventures and followed.

The Great Mother/Father God pleaded with them all to stay, but they ignored the cries and with their free will went on their way. God's heart ached, knowing what the Children were getting into, but, as always, each must experience for themselves, and He must respect that free will that had been given.

Many aeons later one of the Souls who had left Home was sitting in a strange, faraway place and was wondering what was the matter with itself. It had everything it wanted, a home, work and play. It had done everything it could think of and felt satiated and bored with everything. It felt lonely and did not know what it was lonely for.

Its heart ached in a funny way and it felt homesick, but homesick for what? What else was there but life and whatever you could get out of it, one way or the other. Was there something else? Was there something it had known and forgotten about?

If so, then how could it even begin to find its way back. It gave another deep longing sigh.

A million years away in space and yet closer than breath, the Great Mother/Father Being felt the pain and longing of that sigh echo in it's own heart and it knew a great surge of joy. Another one of its long lost children wanted to come Home.

At long last it could lean down and offer a helping hand, a comforting touch and whisper words of guidance and encouragement into a receptive ear. Whatever else its child must endure in order to come Home, it never again need be so lonely. Its cry had been heard and the journey Home had started.

(This was given in meditation and your inner reaction to it will tell you of its truth.)

Belonging

Man's greatest fear – even beyond insecurity, is a fear of loneliness. Man can endure much as long as he does not feel he is completely alone. People want to belong to something. At a very young age a baby will cry if it is left alone, young children like to play with others. In their teens – gangs, clubs, groups, organizations of all kinds are created so that they can feel they belong to something.

Marriage, family extensions, friends. Everyone has within themselves a deep sense of isolation – in spite of numerous other human contacts. Without knowing it we are lonely for God, the ultimate in relationships.

God. It is essential that each man carry his concept of God and his Church within himself. In that way, and that way only wherever he goes and under all circumstances, he can communicate with his God, feel the oneness that exists between them and finally achieve a deep inner peace.

THE REAL LONELINESS

There is a need, that dwells within,
Hidden and almost lost.
We throw away a Paradise,
If only we knew the cost.

We think we need material things,
Or places to go and see.
But the reality need that we always have
Is within; if only we heed.

We need to learn to find our own strength,
With enough to give to others.
Not demand and demand from the folk that we know,
But give to all – as our brothers.

As we painfully give from our lonely hearts,
Not counting the cost or asking for debts.
We will find a just God who pays our dues,
And gives us a Love that just overflows.

For our loneliness comes from a void within,
That no outer can supress,
No man, or woman, child or dog,
No vacation, house or dress.

The void is in Spirit, and Spirit needs God
To heal the lonely wounds.
To fill up with Love from an inner source, so
We can channel to other's demands.

PROJECT

Sometimes when we are feeling at our loneliest, is just the time that we shut ourselves away from everyone and everything and increase the feeling.

Try giving a smile and a quick "Hi" to as many strangers as you can. They will be puzzling afterwards where they know you from, but feeling better at the same time for the acknowledgement.

Another fun exercise is to occasionally say "Hi" to God through the day. Do not automatically assume that God would not want to talk with you – just imagine the smile on HIS face as you thought of Him in the midst of life.

CHAPTER FOURTEEN
Goals

The Seeds of the Future

Our life, this time around and indeed, every time around, has a multiplicity of goals.

We have the goal of understanding

The goal of growth

The goal of learning

The goal of sharing

and the goal of goals – to become one again with our Father and Creator, our Beloved, who, in turn, loves us quite unconditionally.

If you look carefully, everything seems to come in seed form. They even talk about seeding clouds to produce rain. Could it be that God thinks in seed form? Could it be that everything grows from seed, matures and is then allowed to produce other seeds.

So, if we sow the seeds of understanding, growth, learning, sharing, loving and caring, then nurture them, they must grow, mature and produce in that we may be allowed to help others. All of nature assists each other and we are included in that sharing.

What all this means basically is that you can start right where you are, with just a dream, but if you believe in dreams, then things will start to happen. God even dreamed the Universe first.

Responsibility

Through the years, when you searched with a hunger in your soul, although you knew not what you searched for, you assumed that when your search was ended, your problems would also be at an end? Once you had made sense of life on Earth, then you could sit back and take it easy?

But what really happened? You seem to have brewed up more troubles, more responsibilities for yourself, but you know now that you are indeed 'Your brother's keeper'. You are not at all sure that you want that responsibility. After all, you have quite enough troubles of your own without fretting about others. So, what keeps nagging at you, what makes you feel uncomfortable – is it that you are complacent for too long? Can we maybe just turn the clock back and forget the whole business? After all, we have now found, a few kindred souls who are also searching for a deeper meaning to life. We have each other. Why do we have to be responsible for finding any more? Are there any more?

The answer seems to be – yes. There are many more that are lost and away from their real Home. This means that they may have a need. But it is a very special need. You do not have to be qualified in the normal areas to fulfil this particular need. I found, many many years ago, that God put across my path just as many people as I was willing to help, and with just the kinds of needs that I could fulfil. Yet, with my trying to help others I noticed all the time that I benefitted too. It seemed that whatever I did was as if my pouring a jug of healing water over someone, meant that I got splashed too.

Remember you each have words, caring and love to give that no other person can give. Sometimes the people that seem the most self-sufficient to you are those that need that special word, that phone call, that knowing they are wanted. We ALL need to be needed. They by you and you by them. All you have to do is to sit quietly one day and ask God if you can be a co-worker. That sentence, if followed through can transform your life. Think again about what I have suggested you do.

'Ask God if you may be a co-worker?' The idea was put across my path in the book *Initiation* by Elisabeth Haich. Many years ago I did that and first of all, to my amazement the answer was a resounding "Yes!" and secondly, it gave me a personal relationship with God that I could not have achieved in any other way.

I want you to be quite clear as to the terminology of the above sentence. By asking if I could be a co-worker *with* God I was not asking if I could work *for* God, because that would be guessing what God wanted me to do to please Him. This way I quickly found that people were put across my path in the most unusual ways who said they wanted to talk with me and all I had to do was put my ego on one side and inwardly ask for the right words. I would then sometimes hear myself saying things that I had never read about or heard about before, and they were what the person in front of me needed to hear at that particular moment in time. It was amazing to experience and very humbly rewarding.

Goals are made up of 'Todays'

How many of us have, with great enthusiasm, written a long list of New Year's Resolutions on 1st January? How many of us have come across that same list several months later, only to realise that we have not achieved one of them?

One of the problems is that we want to experience the 'goal' NOW. In fact the goal can only be truly experienced, on one day, which is inevitably in the distance. It is hard to visualise that as a reality so we get discouraged and give up.

Goals should be in parts. A and B.

B is the ultimate – the end

A is the path we need to tread to get to B

The path is made up of days, even hours, or even minutes. Over a period of five years I did 800 hours of Spanish.

How? By doing 20 minutes at a time and keeping a record of it. When I had done 3 x 20 minutes it would go on a chart as having done an hour. My chart was on squared paper and drawn like a candle with the goal being able to light the candle. At the end of the five years, I could write some Spanish, read some Spanish and speak a little Spanish, but when they opened their mouths in delight to have a conversation with me I was still lost. They always spoke too fast for me. So I have now switched to German. A waste of five years? No – because it was always good for my concentration skills and learning skills.

I show you a rug that I crocheted and you ask me how long it took me to do. It did not take me four months. It took me 120 'todays'. They were what counted. A few rows each day that added and added. I have slimmed. I did not slim yesterday or last week or even last year. I slimmed in so many 'todays.' The fact that we can split our goals into 'today' segments is what makes it possible for us to achieve so much. So no matter how many years it takes to be a doctor, a teacher or even an orchestra leader, in actual fact it took or takes so many 'todays'.

So – how many years does it take to know God – to feel God in your bones, mind, heart and thoughts. Just one day, because every day of the year is important and has its Value. It is the journey that is important – is part of your future – the journey that you experience here and now – today.

You simply cannot live either yesterday or tomorrow – you can only live today. You cannot live early this morning or late this evening – you can only live now. Everything you experience tomorrow and tomorrow and tomorrow you created 'now'. At the same time, tomorrow is the greatest labour saving device ever invented. So make your goals consist of 'todays' only.

A Path

Books are often needed in the early days of growth in order to give one the understanding of what is available to mankind, yet books, by their very constitution, also prohibit man from experiencing what is really available.

When one reads a book about travelling to the North Pole, if one has a vivid imagination, you can visualise the long dark days, the bitter cold and the stillness, but in no way can it be compared to the experiencing of this. If we read of an adventure, it really belongs to someone else. If we watch an adventure story on TV, it is received by us in diluted form. We must experience things for ourselves in order for them to become real to us, even real memories. If we are really experiencing something it is often scary and we wish we were somewhere else, but afterwards we may say that whilst it was going on we felt truly alive.

So it is with spiritual growth and understanding. We must experience. There is another important factor here. When we read of things, spiritual or otherwise, our experiencing is given to us both by the print and maybe with a bit of extra imagination from us. But if we are experiencing something personally, it has an entirely different feel to it.

Once when on a holiday in Austria on a sunny afternoon, I went for a walk by myself up the side of what I thought was a gentle hill with pine trees. I just wandered up and up avoiding bits of snow and ice that lay around. When I decided it might be time to go down, I was horrified on looking back to see that somehow I had lost the soft earth and was now up on an ice patch too big to get around and I only had slippy-soled casual shoes on. I could no longer see a path at all and it was getting colder and darker.

I quickly had visions of freezing to death overnight. The only sound I could hear way off in the distance was the sound of the ski chairlift which I knew would stop at four o'clock. However, I knew that if I found my way to it, no matter how slippy it was I could then follow the chairs down to the valley.

I headed off in that direction, but suddenly came to a really steep and dark ravine. There was no way around it. It was too steep to walk down and too smooth to climb down. I prayed out loud for some help. Then the idea came to me to sit down and have the courage to allow myself to slide, legs straight out in front of me, down to the next pine tree and then the next and so on. Fortunately I had jeans on. I do not know how long it took me but eventually I did it all the way to the bottom. I was very lucky that the other side was rougher and using all the little pine trees for handholds and footholds, I eventually did crawl and clamber to the top. Across some very icy patches the empty chair lifts were swaying softly in the very cool evening breeze. I did not mind the long slither back down one little bit – I was just so grateful to feel that I was not lost anymore. This happened years ago, but it is as fresh in my memory as if it happened yesterday and in some way I felt as though I had been tested and stretched and not found wanting in faith.

So if we have the courage to try and experience for ourselves – maybe set goals that have no boundaries, there is a breadth and enrichment that comes to life. This is especially true of our spiritual boundaries. Meditation, when done regularly and sincerely can open wide new vistas for us and the goal can be eternity.

Habits

Habits are goals that we have reached and sometimes got stuck with. We don't always want to keep them and we are not always sure how to change them. It is better not to rush the changes, although at the same time, as nature never appears to rush, yet we know that all the time changes are taking place. So we should be open to new learning and understanding all the time yet:-

If rain suddenly pours on to a rock hard field, it will simply pour off again, or sit on the top. However, if the rain is gentle, but persistent, it will gradually soak in and can water the seeds of change that are already lying dormant within.

We may have the habit of gossiping and want to change it. First it comes as an idea in the mind. The next time we might see ourselves gossiping and remind ourselves that we want to stop. The next time we might look rather like a goldfish opening and closing our mouths as we struggle to bring our new goal of 'not gossiping' into fruition. Practice, little by little, day after day and time after time, is what brings about the results – the goals.

PS I was amazed to find that when I decided not to gossip anymore I still had lots to talk about.

PROJECT

Pick one little habit you have that you do not like and begin to practise putting another habit that you do like in its place. Do not just try to squash to death the original habit or take it out leaving a void. It is important to replace it with something positive instead.

CHAPTER FIFTEEN

Our Spiritual Potential

Our Potential

What is the most valuable need we have? A need to know who we really are and what our potential really is. Yet we have to have the faith first of all that there is something different to find out about ourselves and our possibilities.

Yet what did Jesus say, over two thousand years ago: "Seek and Ye shall find, ask and it shall be given unto you, knock and the door will be opened." Do we, or do we not believe in what he said? Too often we do not believe, although many of us are too fearful of the wrath of an avenging God to have the courage to say so.

I was once so incensed with what I thought was the unfairness of God in my life's situation that I threw Him out of the window (so to speak) and stated out loud that I did not want to know Him and I did not believe in Him either, especially as He was supposed to be good. I now jokingly say that about a week later I realised that God seemed to be getting along fine without me and it was me who was still in deep trouble. That was when I began a serious search to find if there was anything else to life, something that had law and order in it like nature does, something that had growth in it, as an acorn holds within itself an oak tree.

Please do believe me when I say that if you have a need to know and understand more of what life is really all about, just ask God in all humility and answers will come.

Faith

You are perfect – now!

You may not know it, but you are in the right spot. You are the right person with the right situations – for Spiritual growth.

I was very overweight for many years. Perfect? Perfect in my understanding to eventually empathise and not just sympathise with other overweight people.

I was ill – Perfect opportunity to learn patience and to give others a chance to give to you.

Divorced? So painful, but perfect opportunity to sit back and see what went wrong with the relationship and what deep, deep lesson was to be learned from it.

To Find A Way

After a certain stage, human beings stop growing physically. From then on their growth is in the realm of experience, thought, sensitivity and awareness – the immaterial dimension.

If we really are the children of God – if God created us from Himself, then what innate powers and abilities do we possess – what potential? If, in addition to God's powers and abilities we have always had free will, then maybe now would be a good time to start accepting responsibility for what happens in our lives. A difficult one, I agree, as we can often see no earthly reason why something is or has happened. Maybe this is because the reason does not stem from this earth life in the first place.

Creativity

Creativity does not necessarily mean to produce something physical such as an embroidery or a piece of woodwork.

We can be creative about our thinking and about our understandings. Open ourselves up to new ideas without fear, knowing we are protected by our inner intuition. Everything starts in your mind first. People are always blaming their circumstances for what they are. They forget they created the circumstances in the first place. They have usually forgotten where and when they created them too, but isn't it better to get up and get busy creating better future circumstances by our positive actions now?

What effect can one person alone create?

This. A scene down by a river. Hundreds of aspen trees along the bank quivering in the sunlight. Very beautiful and peaceful. Suddenly, there up on the cliff side, clinging to a tiny ledge was one aspen tree. Its beauty stood out sharp and clear and was remembered, because it had the courage to step out from the crowd of trees and live in a difficult place, yet because of its courage it was remembered.

ASK AND YOU SHALL RECEIVE

I read a book one winter day,
And my heart was filled with desire
For the book* that I read told of things to be done,
Told of things to which one could aspire.

It told of an order of long ago,
Of people whose forms were fair,
Who asked our God for ways and means,
Responsibilities to bear.

A co-worker* it said was the goal,
A co-worker with God of all.
As I read these words I came alive,
And they pierced right through my soul.

"If you really want to share with us
The burdens and joys of life,
If you learn to float on a pool within,
So you're not touched by all of life's strife.

We have need of people prepared to give,
Whatever their station in life.
No matter how humble, how quiet you are,
You will reflect an inner light."

Initiation by Elisabeth Haich

Try and get at least one of the books I have mentioned – maybe from the library or even secondhand from Amazon.

Books I have personally found inspiring over the years:-

The Aquarian Gospel Of Jesus The Christ by Levi

The Practice Of the Presence Of God
   by Brother Lawrence

Initiation by Elisabeth Haich

Key To Yourself by Venice Bloodworth

As A Man Thinketh by James Alien

Autobiography of a Yogi by Paramahansa Yogananda

THE PRACTICE OF THE SPIRITUAL 'I'

For many years 'I' have lived with 'Me',
A physical body you can touch and see.
Suddenly, with no shadow of doubt
The truth has appeared; what it's all about.

The body we know has eyes and ears,
Laughs at jokes and sometimes has fears,
But who really exists, who truly the one
Most people can't cope with – that sort of sum.

If I lose my hair, or even a limb,
If I lose my teeth, is it such a sin?
Do my friends feel then I have disappeared
So what's the real 'Me'? Now don't be scared.

These days with science – and the way things are,
I can have all new parts with scarcely a scar.
So the physical bits just can't be me;
On that small point I'm sure you'll agree?

Well 'I'm character' then you'll proudly boast,
But characters change from coast to coast.
A weakly man on a journey long,
By the other end, could really be strong.

Forgetting his fears, with friends in need,
He could find the courage to do brave deeds,
From a craven coward to a hero's song.
Which character his, the weak or the strong?

Let us try the idea of a spiritual 'I'
Set in a body with physical eyes.
The spirit is 'I', the body is you,
Now we have a Master and pupil too.

If you can accept that life is a school,
Then you're a wise man and not a fool.
Now with Spirit as Master and body pupil true,
Then adventures abound with successes assured.

* * * * *

FINAL PROJECT

Remember if you begin each day and finish each day with a little prayer and meditation, your life will feel and be so different, even if you do not or cannot step outside the front door.

Remember also that **prayer** is you talking TO God and **meditation** is you listening FOR God. If you practice these things faithfully a new world awaits you – INWARDLY.

I found this saying somewhere many years ago and I think it is very profound:-

"In your silence, God speaks."

THELMA BROWN is available to give lectures and workshops to groups anywhere in the country, and can be contacted at the address at the front of this book or via email :

thelmapatriciabrown@yahoo.co.uk